ABOUT ANIMALS
The 1971 Childcraft Annual

An Annual Supplement to
Childcraft—The How and Why Library

Field Enterprises Educational Corporation
Chicago London Rome Sydney Toronto

Acknowledgments

The publishers of *Childcraft—The How and Why Library*
gratefully acknowledge the courtesy of the following
publishers and organizations. Full illustration
acknowledgments for this volume appear on
pages 328–329.

Wallace Kirkland, *Life* © Time Inc.

Reproduction of painting "Bobwhite" by
Don Richard Eckelberry © Frame House Gallery,
Louisville, Ky.

Preface

Children are fascinated by animals. They'll watch a tiny caterpillar, inching its way along a leaf, with as much interest as they give to a great Bengal tiger, padding about in a zoo. They're as delighted to have a ladybug alight on one of their fingers as they are to have a tame deer nibble corn from their hand. They're brimming with interest and bursting with questions about all of the living, moving creatures of the animal kingdom.

The primary purpose of this book is to heighten that interest and answer many of the questions children ask about animals. Written to hold a child's attention and filled with exciting pictures, it tells about hundreds of kinds of animals—where they live, how they are born, what their food is and how they get it, how they protect or defend themselves, why they do the things they do, and what the world is like for them. All this information has been carefully researched and checked by authorities, for scientific accuracy.

It is hoped that *About Animals* will be an important educational experience that can help a child discover, understand, and gain reverence for, the whole vast, wonderful web of life. Having an interest in animals and really knowing about them can be a source of lifelong pleasure. It can also be a valuable asset. We have just begun to appreciate the tremendous ecological importance of animal life, and to realize that many animals are on the verge of extinction. If we are to save them—and perhaps ourselves and our whole planet, as well—we all need to truly understand and care about animals. And understanding and care must start with today's children who will live in tomorrow's world.

ABOUT ANIMALS

Contents

The Animal Kingdom

A sea gull is an animal.

What's the difference between a pussy willow and a pussy cat?

For a pussy willow, being alive is growing from a seed in the ground. It is having roots to get water from the ground. It is staying in one place, for pussy willows can't move around. It is having green leaves that take in the summer sunlight and use it to make food. It is having seeds from which new pussy willows may grow.

That's the way of pussy willows. They are plants.

For a pussy cat, being alive is being born, and eating, and growing. It is moving around. It is learning about other animals, and playing and making noises. It is growing up and having little kittens.

That's the way of pussy cats. They are animals.

A sea anemone is an animal.

A red fox is an animal.

A kitten is an animal. ▶

Banded Anemone

Is this a flower eating a fish? No,
this is an animal called a
sea anemone eating a fish.

Plant or animal?

Do you know the best way to tell the difference between a plant and an animal? You can't always tell by just looking. Some plants look like animals and some animals look like plants.

At the bottom of the sea, there is a living thing that looks like a flower growing out of the sand. But if a fish swims by and touches the flower's petals, the fish gets caught. A little mouth opens up in the middle of the flower and into it goes the fish!

Do plants have mouths? Can they eat things?

No. No plant in the world has a mouth. And every green plant in the world makes its own food from sunshine, air, and water.

Now the flower on the sea bottom moves. It slides slowly over the sand. Can a plant move?

No. Once a plant sprouts up from its seed it stays in the same place forever unless it is moved by man, an animal, or the wind.

So this living thing at the bottom of the sea is not a plant, because it moves and eats. It is an animal called a sea anemone.

If a living thing moves and eats, it is an animal.

Animals move

If a living thing moves around by itself, it's an animal. Plants can't move by themselves. But animals move in many different ways.

A clam has one foot that it uses for digging into mud or sand.

A penguin walks on two legs.

A kudu walks or runs on four legs.

Ladybugs walk on six legs.

Spiders walk on eight legs.

Centipedes may have as many as a hundred legs on which to walk. And some millipedes walk on more legs than that!

Snakes slide over the ground on no legs at all. They can even climb trees.

Birds, bats, and insects fly. Fish swim.

Some animals move only when they are young. Baby oysters, barnacles, and sponges swim through the water until they find a good place to stay. Then they fasten themselves down and never move again.

Animals are able to move around without help. That's something plants can't do. If it moves by itself, it's an animal.

Centipede

A centipede is an animal that moves on many legs. This centipede has forty legs. Some centipedes have more.

Snakes are animals that have no legs at all. But a snake can move quite fast on rough ground.

California Kingsnake

Gulls

Birds and insects are animals that can use their legs for moving on the ground and their wings for moving in the air.

The kudu is one of the animals that walk and run on four legs.

Greater Kudu

Little wormlike animals live inside these twisty tunnels. They poke their heads up, but they never move around.

Brain Coral

Earthworm

An earthworm makes tunnels in the ground by eating through the dirt. It feeds on bits of plants and leaves in the dirt.

Alfalfa Butterfly

A butterfly's tongue is like a curled tube. It uncurls its tongue and sucks juice from flowers when it is hungry.

Animals eat

If it eats, it's an animal. And there are almost as many ways of eating as there are kinds of animals.

An earthworm eats its way through the ground. It feeds on bits of rotting plants.

A sponge takes in tiny plants and animals from the water that flows through it.

A chameleon shoots out its sticky tongue and catches insects.

A butterfly's tongue is hollow, like a straw. The butterfly keeps its tongue rolled up. When the butterfly gets hungry, it unrolls its tongue. It puts its tongue into a flower and sucks up nectar.

A chipmunk has strong teeth for cracking nuts and seeds. It has pockets in its cheeks. It carries food back to its home in these pockets.

A baleen whale takes a mouthful of seawater with tiny plants and animals in it. It lets the water run out of its mouth. Then it swallows the plants and animals.

Plants make their food from light and water and things in the ground and air. But animals must eat to live.

Sponge

Many little tunnels in a sponge's body
let in seawater. In the water are tiny
plants and animals the sponge eats.

The chipmunk's cheeks are full
of nuts and seeds to carry
home. It cracks the shells
with its strong teeth.

Chipmunk

New living things

All living things come from other living things. Every baby animal comes from a grown-up animal like itself. A baby penguin comes from a penguin. A horse comes from a horse. A beetle comes from a beetle.

Some baby animals come right out of their mothers' bodies. Horses are born this way. So are monkeys, cats, whales, and some fish and snakes.

Some baby animals come out of eggs that come from their mothers' bodies. Penguins are born this way. So are beetles, frogs, and most fish.

Some baby animals look like their parents. Some look very different. But every baby animal grows up to be exactly the same kind of animal as its parents.

Emperor Penguins

The baby penguin came from an egg that was laid by a grown-up mother penguin. The baby will grow to look just like her.

The baby beetle, at left, is very different from the adult. But when the baby grows up, it will look like the adult.

Baby and Adult Mexican Bean Beetles

The colt came out of its mother's body. It looks very much like her.

Mare and Colt

Lions

As the lion cub grows up, it will learn from its mother and father many things about being a lion.

An animal grows up

Could a parrot ever roar like a lion? Could a frog learn to fly like a bird? Could a lion crack seeds as a parrot does?

None of these things could ever happen. Each baby animal grows up to live the way its parents live. It will look and act and sound like the animals of its own kind, and like no others.

A lion cub learns to walk and then run. It learns to eat meat. It growls, then it roars. It learns to hunt other animals for food.

The frog grows up and does all the things frogs do. It hops and croaks and catches insects with its sticky tongue.

The parrot learns to fly. It easily cracks nuts and seeds with its bill. It squawks with its noisy voice.

Each animal learns to live the life that all animals of its kind live. Each animal does the things it must do to stay alive. That's the way of animals.

Macaw

A parrot learns to live the way all parrots live. It flies, eats nuts and seeds, and squawks with its noisy voice.

A frog jumps and swims and croaks because its body is made to do such things. The frog can't act any other way.

Green Frog

Margay Wildcat

Animals are everywhere

. . . leaping, creeping, running, and walking
in forests, deserts, meadows, and snowy places.

Raccoons

Bat-Eared Fox

Ribbon Seal

Kassala Goats

Jaguarundi and Boa Constrictor

Animals are everywhere

. . . swimming, splashing, and floating
in oceans, lakes, rivers, and ponds.

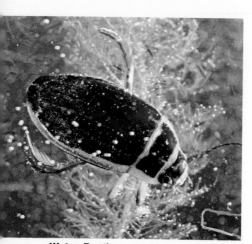

Water Beetle

Clown Sea Slug

Painted Turtles

Dolphin

Mandarin Duck

Animals are everywhere

. . . buzzing and flapping and fluttering
above the ground.

Animals are everywhere

. . . digging, squirming, and sliding
below the ground.

Mole Cricket

Pocket Gopher

Mole

Bobcat

Animals are everywhere

. . . on high mountaintops . . .

Mountain Goat

Bats

Animals are everywhere

. . . in dark holes and caves.
Animals are everywhere!

Cave Cricket

Cave Salamander

Animal classes

To make it easier to study animals, scientists have arranged all animals into classes. An animal class is made up of animals that are all alike in important ways.

There are many kinds of animal classes and each one has a name. Every kind of animal belongs to one of the classes. These pages show the kinds of animals that belong to each of the six most important classes.

Mammals

If an animal drinks milk when it's a baby, and has hair on its body, it belongs to the mammal class.

Birds

If an animal comes out of an egg with a hard shell, and has feathers on its body, it belongs to the class of birds.

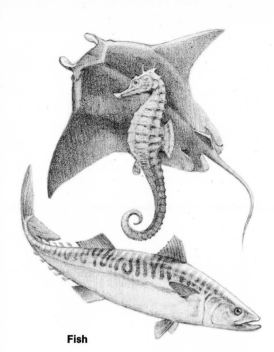

Fish

If an animal lives in water,
and has gills and scales and
fins on its body, it belongs
to the class of fish.

Reptiles

If an animal has a scaly skin,
is cold-blooded, and is always
born on the land, it belongs
to the class of reptiles.

Arthropods

If an animal has more than
four jointed legs and a hard
covering over its whole body,
it belongs to the class of
arthropods.

Amphibians

If an animal is born in water
and breathes with gills, but
can live on land when it grows
up, it belongs to the class
of amphibians.

It's a Mammal

The zebra is a mammal.

Do you have a pet mammal? If you have a dog or cat you have a mammal. Hamsters and gerbils and guinea pigs are mammals, too. And so are you!

Maybe you've seen a cow feeding her calf. The calf drank milk from its mother's body. Of all the animals, only mammals do this.

Mammals are warm-blooded. The day may be freezing cold or very hot but mammals' bodies stay at just about the same temperature all the time.

Mammals have fur or hair. The fur can be short or long, straight or curly, soft or hard. There may be lots of it, or just a few thick, stiff hairs.

There are more than 800,000 kinds of insects and more than 30,000 kinds of fishes. There are only about 5,000 kinds of mammals. But of all the animals, mammals are the ones we most often choose for our pets and helpers.

The mountain lion is a mammal.

The walrus is a mammal. ▶

Two mammals

This is a looking page. There are lots of things to see in this picture of a mother giraffe and her baby.

The mother giraffe has a very long neck. You might think there would be a lot of bones in such a long neck. But the mother giraffe has no more bones in her neck than you have in yours! Her bones are just longer.

The mother giraffe's long neck and long legs make her very tall. Giraffes are the tallest of all animals.

The two giraffes have spots and squiggles on their bodies. These spots help the giraffes hide. When a giraffe goes into a bunch of trees, the spots on its body look just like leaves. It's very, very hard to see a giraffe when it hides among trees.

The two giraffes have tails with big bunches of fur on the ends. The giraffes use their tails to brush away flies and other insects. The giraffes' bodies are covered with smooth fur. Giraffes are mammals and all mammals have some fur or hair on their bodies.

Blotched Giraffes

Mammal babies

Is a mouse like a moose? Or a dolphin like a deer? Or a bat like a cat?

These animals seem to be quite different from each other. But they are all alike in one important way. They are all mammals. That means they're all born the same way, and they all eat the same kind of food when they are babies.

Most mammal babies live inside their mothers before they are born. The baby is joined to its mother by a tube. The baby gets food and oxygen from the mother's body through the tube. The baby lives and grows and when its body is ready, the baby comes out of the mother's body.

Different kinds of baby birds eat different kinds of things. So do baby fish, reptiles, insects, and amphibians.

Newborn meadow mice are not much bigger than a thimble. Their eyes are closed and they are weak and helpless.

Meadow Mice

But all baby mammals eat the same thing. They all eat milk that comes from their mothers' bodies. Baby lions eat milk. Baby mice eat milk. Baby whales eat milk. Baby bats eat milk. No baby mammal ever eats anything else until it begins to grow up.

Many kinds of mammal babies are weak and helpless for a long time. Kittens, puppies, mice, and human babies, which are mammals too, are born with weak legs and closed eyes. But some mammal babies are stronger. A moose calf can walk with its mother after just a few days. A pronghorn antelope can run 25 miles an hour when it is only a day old.

Mammal babies are different in many ways. But in the way they are born and in the food they eat, they are all alike.

A baby moose is born with its eyes open. It can walk in just a few hours.

Moose

Great Gray Kangaroo

Pouch babies

A newborn kangaroo is only about an inch long. A koala is less than an inch long. And an opossum is smaller still—smaller than a bee.

These are the most helpless of the mammal babies. They spend their first months in their mothers' pouches. They don't move out of the pouches. They don't even peek out. They just drink milk and grow.

Then for a few weeks or months they play jack-in-the-box games with their mothers. They spend part of the time out of the pouch. But they hurry back inside when they are afraid of something.

After they leave the pouches, the babies stay close to their mothers.

Opossum babies go with their mother when she looks for food. They ride on her back.

The koala baby rides piggyback, too. The mother moves through the treetops eating leaves. The baby hangs on tight. It stays with its mother until it is about a year old.

The kangaroo baby is called a joey. He outgrows his pouch when he is about 10 months old. Then he hops along beside his mother. He stays with her until he is about 18 months old.

Although these babies are tiny and weak at first, they grow into quite large, strong animals. The full grown opossum is about as big as a cat. The full grown koala is about as long as a yardstick. The kangaroo, when it is grown, is biggest of all. It becomes nearly as tall as a short man.

A baby koala rides piggy back wherever its mother goes.

Koala

A mother opossum takes her whole family for a ride.

Virginian Opossum

How mammal babies grow

The newborn meadow mouse weighs little more than a feather. Its eyes are closed and it has no fur.

The baby river otter's eyes are closed, too. But a thick fur coat covers its body.

The fawn's eyes are open. Its mother has hidden it in the bushes until it can walk. Spots on its body make it look like part of the bushes. It has no smell. A bear can walk right past and not see or smell the baby fawn.

Ten days pass. The meadow mouse now has a fur coat. Its eyes are open and it can run. It is almost grown up.

The river otter baby is still helpless. Its eyes are still closed.

The fawn can walk now. It follows its mother.

Bear and Fawn

The newborn fawn keeps still and quiet so the bear won't see it.

River Otters

Mother and her babies have just
had a swim.

A month passes. The baby otter opens its eyes. The
meadow mouse is full grown. It even has babies of its
own!

Six months pass. The fawn's spots are gone now. A
bear can see it and smell it. But the fawn can run swiftly
on strong legs.

The baby otter has become a champion swimmer. It
loves to dive and splash and play in the water. Again and
again it slides down a muddy bank into the river.

At the end of a year the fawn and the otter are nearly
full grown. But the meadow mouse's life is nearly over.
Each mammal baby grows its own way at its own speed.

What does it eat?

The biggest difference between mammals and all other kinds of animals is—milk! Mammal mothers feed their babies milk that comes from the mothers' bodies. No other animals can do this—only mammals.

So the first food of every baby mammal is its mother's milk. Baby buffaloes and bear cubs, skunks and squirrels, whales and walruses all drink milk.

As a baby mammal grows, its jaws get strong. Its baby teeth fall out, and stronger, sharper teeth grow in their place. The little mammal learns to bite and tear and gnaw and chew. Then it needs more than milk.

Antelopes and gazelles need grass.

Giraffes and elephants need leaves.

Wolf pups and lion cubs need meat.

An anteater licks up termites and ants with its sticky tongue.

Giant Anteater

African Lions

Very young lion cubs drink milk.
Later they learn to eat meat.

American Bison

A baby bison drinks milk, too. When
it is older it will eat grass.

Some babies follow their mother and eat the same things she eats. But some babies need to be taught how to eat grown-up food.

A father wolf goes hunting and when he comes back, he spits out meat near his pups. The pups play with it, then they taste it. They find they like this kind of food. They become meat-eaters and never drink milk again.

Lion cubs follow their mother when she hunts. She lets them play with the animal she has killed. Once the cubs taste the meat, they learn to like it.

Every baby mammal drinks milk for a while after it is born. But as the babies grow up, they learn to eat the kind of food their mothers and fathers do.

Hippopotamus Mother and Baby

Learning days

When a baby hippopotamus starts to walk, its mother bumps it with her big nose to make it stay close behind her. She can protect it better that way. Soon, the baby learns to walk behind its mother wherever they go.

Learning to stay behind its mother is just one of many things a baby hippopotamus must learn. Baby days are learning days for hippos and all other mammals. That's when they learn the things that will help them stay alive as babies and as grown-ups.

Different kinds of mammal babies learn different ways of life. Seals, which will spend most of their lives in water, learn to swim by riding on their mothers' backs. Lion cubs, which will live by hunting, watch their mothers hunt. Baby bears learn what's good for them to eat by seeing their mother gobble berries and snatch fish out of streams.

The baby mammal learns from its mother. Most mammal mothers don't really try to teach things to their babies—animals aren't that smart. But the babies watch their mother and do the things they see her do.

A day comes when the baby mammal is nearly grown-up. Then its mother may drive it away. That's what mother bears, moose, and beavers do. But the young mammal is ready to live its own life. It has learned how to find food and how to keep out of danger. It has learned how to stay alive.

Timber Wolves and Rabbit

Wolf cubs learn to hunt by watching an older wolf.

Where the mammals are

Mammals are everywhere. Polar bears, musk oxen, walruses, and reindeer live in some of the coldest parts of the world. Camels and kangaroo rats live in some of the warmest places. Little pikas and ground squirrels live on mountaintops. Gophers and moles live underground. Mammals make their homes in hot, tropical jungles and cool, northern forests. Whales, dolphins, and porpoises are mammals that spend their whole lives in the ocean.

Wherever there's a place to live, mammals have moved in.

Polar Bear

Some mammals live in cold, snowy places.

Rhesus Monkey

Some mammals live in hot,
damp jungles.

Arabian Camel

Some mammals live in hot,
dry deserts.

Some mammals live in
dark caves and can fly.

Bechstein's Bat

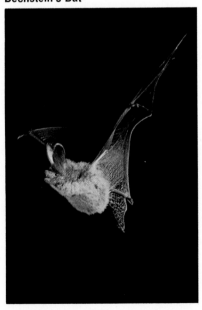

Some mammals live in
the ocean.

Dolphin

Animal houses

Where do the animals go when winter winds blow, when snow is in the air and on the ground? Where do they hide when it's wet outside? Are little animals out when dangerous animals are about?

Some mammals need no house of any kind. Whales do not. Neither do many of

An underwater tunnel leads into the house where beavers sleep and stay warm.

Beaver Home

the hoofed animals, such as moose and musk oxen.

Some mammals look for shelter only at night or when they are having their young. Most monkeys sleep in trees. The elephant looks for a hidden spot to have her baby.

But some mammals make houses to keep out the sun or the wind or snow or other animals. The prairie dog digs a burrow with many rooms. The prairie is hot, but the burrow is cool. It is safe, too. Around the doorways are heaps of dirt. The prairie dog sits on these to look around for danger. The dirt heaps also keep out floods.

In winter, the fox is safe in his burrow deep in a sandy bank. If snow covers one, two, three doorways, he can go out through four or five others. The muskrat's summer home of wet grass and weeds turns into a winter home of ice.

The beaver makes a house of branches and twigs. The house is usually in a pond. The top of the house freezes in winter. Wind and snow and hungry animals can't get in. But the bottom of the house doesn't freeze. The beaver goes in and out to get the food he has stored at the bottom of the pond. An animal's house of whatever kind is just right for the animal that lives in it.

Squirrel Home

Some squirrels have homes in hollow trees where they store food for the winter.

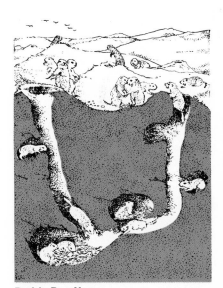

Prairie Dog Home

A prairie dog sleeps and stores food in little rooms around a tunnel.

The life of a black bear

Near winter's end, three bear cubs were born in their mother's dark, warm den. Now it's spring and their mother brings them out to see the world.

There are many exciting new things for the cubs to see and smell. Mother bear watches her babies carefully.

While mother eats nearby, the cubs play. They snap and growl and slap each other with their paws.

After mother bear finishes eating, she feeds the babies. Like all baby mammals, the little cubs drink milk.

The cubs learn about water in a mud hole. Later, they will learn that good-tasting fish are in the water.

Turn the page to see the rest of this picture story.

The cubs learn to climb trees. This cub
crawled out on a branch and went
to sleep in the warm, summer sun.

Summer is coming to an end. Soon,
the cubs and their mother will go back
to the den for their long winter sleep.

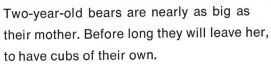

Two-year-old bears are nearly as big as
their mother. Before long they will leave her,
to have cubs of their own.

Black Bears

The bald eagle is a bird.

It's a Bird

Do you know what makes a bird different from any other animal?

Not its wings. Some other animals have wings, too.

Not its bill. Some other animals have bills, too.

Not its eggs. Many other animals lay eggs.

Give up?

Feathers! All birds have feathers. And birds are the only animals that have feathers.

So if it has feathers—it's a bird!

The peacock is a bird.

The toucan is a bird. ▶

The hummingbird is a bird.

This bird

This is a looking page. What do you see when you look at this blue jay?

Its wings are stretched out. The feathers overlap. Because they overlap, the feathers catch and hold the air. They help the bird fly.

The bird's tail feathers overlap, too. They help the bird steer itself when it flies, and they help the bird land.

The bird has claws on its feet. The claws help the bird perch on the birch log.

If you could touch this bird, you would find that it has two kinds of feathers. The feathers you see are stiff. Under these, next to the bird's skin, is a layer of soft feathers called *down*. Down helps keep the bird warm. Some birds line their nests with down.

Blue Jay

Ostriches

The baby ostrich on the left has been
out of its egg for several minutes.
Its feathers are beginning to dry.
The other baby ostrich is just breaking out of its egg. In a moment, it
will push itself all the way out.

Coming out of the egg

Inside its egg the tiny baby bird lies curled up in a ball. Its head is bigger than its body. Its eyes are closed. All of the food it will need is inside the egg.

The baby bird grows until it fills the whole inside of the egg. Then it is ready to hatch.

On the baby bird's bill is a tiny tooth. The bird uses this tooth to get out of the egg. The tooth falls off a few days after a baby bird leaves its egg.

When the baby is ready to hatch, it begins to move inside the egg. The eggshell cracks. The baby bird scrapes its tooth against the crack and the crack grows bigger. Pieces of the shell fall off.

After a while the baby bird has made a big hole in the shell. The baby bird wiggles through the hole. A new life has come into the world.

Baby birds

Some baby robins lie close together in a nest. Their eyes are closed. They have no feathers. They can't stand on their tiny, weak legs.

With a flutter of wings the mother robin lands on the nest. In her bill is a wiggling worm. At once, each baby's mouth opens wide. "Me! Me! Give it to me!" each open mouth seems to be saying.

The mother pushes the worm into a mouth and flies away. She'll be back soon with another worm or insect. Then another baby bird will have its turn to eat.

On a pile of grass near a river are some baby ducks. They are different from the robins. The little ducks have fuzzy feathers. Their bright eyes are wide open. And when their mother quacks, they follow her out of the nest. All in a row they waddle to the river for a swim.

Some kinds of birds, such as robins, blue jays, and nuthatches, are helpless long after they hatch. But other kinds of birds, such as flamingos, ducks, chickens, and geese, can see and walk and care for themselves soon after they hatch.

Robins

Baby robins are weak and helpless. Their parents have to feed them.

A baby flamingo leaves its nest three or four hours after it hatches.

Flamingos

Birds that fly and birds that don't

A baby swift is getting ready to fly. Ever since it hatched, its feathers have been getting longer. Its wings have been growing stronger. Now, the little bird is ready.

It hops to the edge of the nest. Even though it has never flown, the swift knows just what to do. It spreads its wings and pushes itself off the nest with its legs. Air pushes up on the swift's wings and holds the little bird up. The swift flaps its wings. Feathers on the ends of the wings spread out and twist. This pulls air under each wing and pulls the baby swift forward.

Baby swifts, swallows, woodpeckers, and many other birds can fly well the very first time they try. But some birds, such as sparrows, need a little practice first. They flutter weakly out of the nest. Then they hop about on the ground, flapping their wings for a few days before they can really fly.

Swifts and sparrows and all the other birds you see every day can fly. So it may surprise you to learn that there are some birds that *can't* fly!

Ostriches can't fly. Their wings are just too small to lift their big bodies into the air.

Penguins can't fly. Their wings are like a seal's flippers. Penguins use their wings for swimming. Penguins can swim as well as fish can.

And the birds called kiwis can't fly. They have no wings.

Some of the flying birds are the fastest of all animals. The fastest bird is the duck hawk. It can fly 175 miles an hour!

Chimney Swift

Most birds can fly.

This bird can't fly.

Kiwi

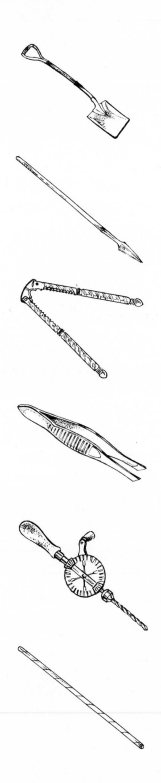

Shovels, spears, and nutcrackers

A roseate spoonbill wades by the seashore with its head under water. Its bill is like a shovel. It swings its head from side to side and shovels tiny fish and other food from the mud and water.

A heron's bill is like a spear. It is long and pointed. A heron sticks its sharp bill into fish, lifts them out of the water and swallows them.

A parrot's bill is like a nutcracker. A parrot can easily crack open nuts and seeds with its big, strong bill.

Robins' and sparrows' bills are like tweezers. Robins and sparrows eat things they find on the ground. Their bills make it easy to pick up things.

A woodpecker's bill is like a drill. A woodpecker eats insects that live under the bark of trees. The woodpecker pounds its bill against a tree and the sharp, pointed bill makes a hole in the bark. Then the woodpecker can get at the insects.

A hummingbird's bill is like a soda straw. It is a long, hollow tube. The hummingbird sticks its long bill deep into a flower and sips up nectar.

Most birds bills are special tools. They are shaped to help the bird get the kind of food it eats.

Blue Parrot

Hummingbird

Savannah Sparrow

Roseate Spoonbill

Louisiana Heron

Woodpecker

Oriole Nest

Robin Nest

Homes for baby birds

Nests are the homes that birds make for their babies. The mother bird lays her eggs in the nest and the babies grow up in it. Then all the birds leave the nest.

Different kinds of birds make different kinds of nests. Robins make nests like bowls, out of anything they can use—grass, twigs, leaves, string. They line the insides of the bowls with mud. Then they cover the mud with bits of grass.

Pied-billed grebes make nests that float. They make the nests of water plants and reeds, and fasten them to plants growing in lakes and ponds.

Grebe Nest

Barn Swallow Nests

Barn swallows make nests like little round pots of mud and straw. Ducks make piles of grass on the ground and line them with feathers that they pull out of their bodies. Ovenbirds make dome-shaped nests of leaves and grass. The nests look somewhat like old-fashioned ovens. The ovenbird got its name from the kind of nest it builds.

Some birds don't build their own nests. Some kinds of parrots just lay their eggs in hollow places in tree trunks. And cowbirds and European cuckoos lay their eggs in the nests of other birds!

Eider Duck Nest

Yellow Parrot Nest

The life of a Canada goose

In early spring a pair of Canada geese pick each other as mates. The female, at left, will soon lay eggs.

The female makes a nest of grass and feathers. She nestles on her eggs, warming them.

Look out! An animal is nearby.
The goose beats her wings,
hisses, and honks. This
frightens the animal away.

Nearly a month passes. Then
the wet, weak little goslings
push out of their eggs into
the world.

Turn the page to see
the rest of this picture story.

The life of a Canada goose

The goslings can walk almost at once. After a day, they leave the nest to look around.

Goslings swim and dive without being taught. Their parents protect them as they swim.

The 2-week-old goslings waddle about from place to place, learning about life.

Now, summer is nearly over.
The goslings are 2 months old—
nearly old enough to fly.

In the fall, families of geese
make ready to fly south. Next
year, the young geese will be
ready to have families of
their own.

It's a Fish

Sometimes it's hard to tell what's fish and what isn't. A sea horse doesn't look like a fish, but it is. And a dolphin looks like a fish, but isn't!

How can you tell if an animal is a fish? Well, nearly all fish have scales. Scales are little round or diamond-shaped pieces of thin bony stuff. They fit together over the fish's whole body.

And nearly all fish have fins. A fish usually has a fin on its back, a fin on its belly, a broad fin for a tail, and two fins on each side.

And all fish have gills. Gills are slits in a fish's head, behind its mouth. Fish breathe with gills.

Scales, fins, and gills—if it has all these things, it's a fish!

A sea horse is a fish.

A perch is a fish.

An eel is a fish.

This is a triggerfish. ▶

This fish

This is a looking page. What does the picture tell you about the fish?

This fish has shiny scales. Scales are like small, thin pieces of fingernail that cover a fish's body.

This fish has big, staring eyes. Its eyes are always open because it has no eyelids.

This fish has fins on its back and underside. The fish steers itself with its fins as it swims. It swims by wiggling its broad tail.

On the fish's head, just above the front fins, are the fish's gills. Every fish has gills.

Gills are what a fish breathes with. They are openings filled with thin pieces of skin like the pages of a book. Water goes into the openings and through the "pages." They take the oxygen out of the water and put the oxygen into the fish's blood. Like all animals, a fish must have oxygen to live.

Brown Trout

Champion egg layers

Some fish don't lay eggs. Some fish lay a few eggs. But some fish lay thousands of eggs. And some fish lay millions of eggs!

A mother herring lays more than thirty thousand eggs at a time. The eggs drop down in the water and stick to sand, rocks, or plants. A mother sardine may lay as many as a hundred thousand eggs. Her eggs float in the water.

But the champion egg layers are cod and turbot. One mother cod will lay as many as four million eggs. And a mother turbot lays as many as nine million eggs.

With millions of fish laying millions of eggs, you might think the oceans, lakes, and rivers would be filled with baby fish. But most fish eggs never hatch. Fish eggs have no shells to protect them. They are round and soft like bits of jelly. Many eggs wash ashore and dry up. Many are gobbled up by other fish. Only a few eggs out of every million ever become baby fish.

Jewel Cichlids

This fish lays hundreds of eggs
that stick to rocks and sand.
Some fish lay millions of eggs
that float in the water.

Finny fathers

In the world of fish, it's the father that does most of the baby sitting.

A father smallmouth black bass starts to take care of his babies even before they're hatched. He makes a wide, saucer-shaped hole in the sand. The mother bass lays her eggs in the hole. The eggs are sticky. They stick to the sand and do not float away.

After the mother lays the eggs the father pushes her away. He wants to guard the eggs all by himself. He swims back and forth over the nest. He fans the eggs

A father sea horse
keeps the mother's eggs
in a pouch on his stomach.

When the eggs hatch,
baby sea horses shoot out of
their father's pouch.

Sea horse

Stickleback

This fish is guarding eggs in a nest.

with his tail. This keeps the water around the eggs fresh and helps them hatch.

When the babies hatch they cannot swim well at first. The father watches over them. He fights anything that comes near. When the babies can swim, the father swims with them and guards them while they find food.

Many other father fish make nests and guard their babies as a father smallmouth black bass does. But a father sea catfish protects his babies in a different way. He keeps the eggs in his mouth until they hatch. When they hatch, he holds the babies in his mouth until they're big enough to take care of themselves. Then he spits them out into the water and away they swim.

Fish food

Nearly everything that lives in the water is food for a hungry fish.

In the ocean, most fish eat only other fish. Ocean cod, hake, tarpon, and tuna dine on smaller herrings, sardines, and anchovies. And the big fish are themselves gulped down by sharks. Sharks will eat any animal, dead or alive.

In rivers and lakes, fish eat fish, too. But some of them add other tasty things to their fish diet. Trout jump out of the water to snap at flying insects. Sturgeons dine on snails, crayfish, and insects. Big, hungry bass, pike, and bowfins gobble up frogs, baby ducks, and even baby muskrats.

Some kinds of fish eat only plants. Carp and sucker-mouth catfish swim along at the bottom of rivers and ponds. With tiny teeth they chew up bits of plants that grow in the mud.

A few kinds of fish eat both plants and animals. Parrot fish eat seaweed and tiny worms that live in coral. The ocean sunfish eats tiny shrimps, baby fish, jellyfish, and tiny plants called algae.

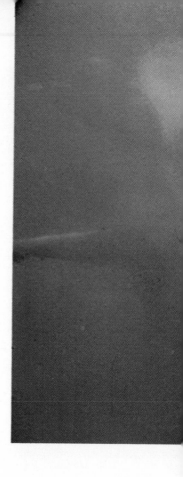

Great Blue Shark Feeding on Dead Bottle-nosed Whale

Freshwater Fish

Brook Trout

Northern Pike

Largemouth Black Bass

Carp

Mudskippers

Archerfish

Which is the strangest fish?

There are thousands of kinds of fishes. If you tried to choose the strangest fish in the world, you'd have a hard time.

The mudskipper has a frog head and a fish body. It often crawls onto land and hops about. It can jump up and catch flying insects in its mouth.

An archerfish shoots its food. The archerfish swims at the top of the water. A beetle comes buzzing past. The fish shoots a stream of water from its mouth. The water hits the beetle and it falls down. The archerfish gobbles it up.

There's a fish called a cowfish. It has horns on its head.

There's a fish called an elephant-nose mormyrid. Its long nose looks like an elephant's trunk.

A puffer fish can fill itself with air. It looks like a round balloon with eyes and a mouth.

Leafy sea dragons look like pieces of seaweed. A flounder has both eyes on one side of its body. You can see the insides of a glass catfish.

These are just a few of the strange fish that live in the world. See what a hard time you'd have trying to choose the strangest?

Cowfish

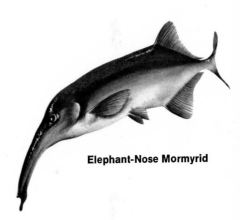

Elephant-Nose Mormyrid

Southern Puffer

Grunts, croaks, snores, and roars

The ocean is a noisy place! It's full of grunts, croaks, squeaks, snores, clicks, and roars. Many of these sounds are made by fish.

Some fish are named after the sounds they make. One kind of fish rubs its teeth together to make a grunting noise. So the fish is called a grunt.

Another kind of fish makes a croaking noise that sounds like *boop-boop-boop-boop*. That fish is called a croaker. And can you guess what kind of noise is made by the fish called a snorer?

Pollack, haddock, toadfishes, and many other fish also make grunting noises. They grunt by snapping some of their muscles against a piece of skin inside their bodies. Sea horses make a clicking noise by hitting a piece of bone on their heads against a piece of bone on their backs.

Sharks sometimes make a roaring noise. But they aren't really roaring—they're burping! Many sharks swallow air to keep their bodies up near the top of the water. When they want to go deeper they have to burp up the air. The burp sounds like a roar.

Noises such as the shark's roar have no meaning. But some fish noises seem to mean something. Many of them seem to be made by male fish calling to female fish. Some of them are made by fish getting ready to fight. Scientists study fish noises to see if all these grunts, croaks, and clicks mean anything.

Toadfish

The toadfish makes a noise by
snapping one of its muscles
against a piece of skin.

The grunt gets its name from
the grunting noise it makes
by rubbing its teeth together.

White Grunts

It's a Reptile

Suppose you found some leathery, rubbery eggs on the ground. And suppose that little scaly-skinned animals hatched out of the eggs. Do you know what kind of animals they would be?

They could only be reptiles. Fish have scaly skins—but fish can't lay eggs on land. Birds lay eggs on land—but birds don't have scaly skins. Only reptiles have scaly skins *and* lay eggs on the land.

Snakes, turtles, lizards, tuataras, alligators, and crocodiles are reptiles.

A crocodile is a reptile.

A green sea turtle is a reptile.

A gila monster is a reptile.

This reptile is a python. ▶

This reptile

This is a looking page. Look at this turtle.

The turtle's head looks as if an artist had painted stripes and spots on it. That's why this kind of turtle is called a painted turtle.

The turtle's shell looks hard and shiny and bumpy. When the turtle fears danger it pulls its head, legs, and tail into the shell. The shell is too hard for most animals to bite through. So when the turtle hides in its shell it is usually safe.

Look at the turtle's toes. On each toe there is a sharp little claw. The turtle's feet are webbed. Do you think this helps the turtle swim better?

The turtle looks as if it is getting ready to go into the water. It doesn't look as if it could swim well because of its hard, heavy shell. But this kind of turtle is a good swimmer.

Painted Turtle

Meet the reptiles

You can always tell a turtle by its shell. A box turtle has a high, round shell that it can close up like a box. A map turtle has a wide, flat shell with bumpy edges. A soft-shelled turtle's shell looks like a green pancake. But all turtles have shells. And most turtles can pull their heads, legs, and tails into their shells at the first sign of danger.

Another reptile that is easy to tell is the snake. Whether it's a little, 15-inch-long ringneck snake or a big, 30-foot anaconda, every snake has the same kind of shape—long, round, and legless.

Mud Turtles

If these baby turtles see an enemy they will pull themselves into their shells.

Garter snakes are harmless to people. They eat worms, frogs, toads, and insects.

Garter Snake

Sometimes it's hard to tell what's a lizard and what isn't. There are lizards that look like snakes and lizards that look like worms. And alligator lizards look like baby alligators. But there's one way to tell geckos, skinks, and some other lizards. If an animal grabs one of these lizards by the tail—the tail comes off and the lizard runs away! It doesn't hurt these lizards to lose their tails. And they soon grow new ones!

Alligators and crocodiles are two reptiles that look much alike. But an alligator has fatter, shorter jaws, and is smaller. The crocodile is the biggest of all the reptiles.

Gecko

It doesn't hurt this lizard to have its tail break off. It soon grows a new tail.

An alligator lies in the sun during the day and hunts for food at night.

Alligator

Scaly babies and mothers

A big brown American alligator crawls into some thorny bushes. She pulls up bushes with her mouth. She stamps her feet. Soon, she has made a wide, clear place. She makes a pile of mud and plants. She scoops a hole in the top of the pile and lays as many as fifty eggs in the hole. Then she covers the eggs with mouthfuls of mud and plants.

For two months the mother alligator stays by her nest. One day she hears little grunting noises. She tears the nest open with her teeth. Tiny baby alligators blink at the sudden bright sunshine.

Alligators take care of their eggs until they hatch. But most reptile mothers just lay their eggs and leave. Their babies never see them.

Mother turtles dig holes in mud or sand. They lay their eggs in the holes. Then they cover up the eggs and go away. The warm sun hatches the eggs. The baby turtles dig their way out of the nest and crawl to the water.

Most mother snakes just lay their eggs and crawl away, too. But a few kinds of snakes wrap themselves around their eggs until they hatch. When the eggs hatch, the mothers leave.

A mother alligator puts her eggs inside a nest of mud and grass. When the eggs hatch, the mother tears the nest open.

American Alligators

New skins for old

A shiny garter snake wiggles through the grass. Its wrinkled old skin hangs from the tip of its tail. The snake comes to some rocks. It slides between them. The old skin catches on one of the rocks. With a twist of its tail, the snake crawls on. The old skin stays behind.

Every few months a snake grows too big for its skin. Each time, it gets rid of its old skin by crawling right out of it.

When the old skin is ready to come off, it dries up and becomes loose. The snake rubs its mouth against something rough. The skin around its lips splits and opens up. This doesn't hurt the snake.

The snake starts to crawl. As it crawls, its old skin turns inside out and slides down the snake's body. At last, the old skin just hangs from the snake's tail. The snake crawls between some rocks or some branches. Off comes the old skin. Away crawls the snake in a shiny new skin that grew beneath the old one.

Lizards take off their old skins, too. But because of their legs, they can't get the skins off in one piece as a snake can. The lizards tear off their old skins in pieces. And some lizards eat the pieces.

Eastern Timber Rattlesnake

This snake has just crawled
out of its old skin. Its new
skin is bright and shiny.

A lizard tears its old skin
off in pieces. Some lizards
eat their old skins!

Gecko

Suppers for snakes

Snakes eat only live food. Most snakes eat rats, birds, lizards, and rabbits. Small snakes eat mice, worms, frogs, snails, and insects. Snakes called hook-nosed snakes eat mostly spiders. African egg-eating snakes eat only birds' eggs.

But guess what the favorite food of some snakes is? It's other snakes! Black racer snakes eat more snakes than any other kind of food. King snakes and cobras eat lots of other snakes, too.

Snakes don't chew their food. They swallow it whole. Snakes can open their mouths very wide. Their heads and bodies stretch to let in big things.

Egg-eating snakes can swallow eggs that are bigger than their heads.

Little garter snakes can swallow whole frogs.

And big pythons can swallow whole hogs, small deer, or goats, hoofs and all!

Snakes can swallow things that are bigger than their heads. This snake is going to swallow a chicken egg.

The snake's jaws are able to come apart and its skin stretches. The water in its mouth makes the egg slippery so it slides in easily.

The egg slides down the snake's throat. A bone in the snake's throat will crack the shell. Then the snake will spit out the pieces.

African Egg-Eating Snake

Moving without legs

Snakes have no legs at all, but they move quite well without them. A snake can go zig-zagging over the ground just about as fast as you can walk.

Most snakes leave a wiggly trail when they crawl. They do this because they curve their bodies into one S shape after another. The top, middle, and bottom parts of the S push against the ground. This makes the snake slide forward.

The sidewinder snake moves sideways. It folds itself up like a spring. Then it stretches its head out as far as it can and lays it on the ground. It pushes hard against the ground and pulls the rest of its body alongside its head. Each time the sidewinder pulls itself sideways, its body leaves the ground a little way. So the sidewinder is really hopping along instead of crawling along! Instead of leaving a wiggly trail, it leaves a trail like a row of I's.

Some snakes crawl on the large, flat scales of their undersides. Pythons and rattlers and boas do this. They push the scales forward. The scales dig into the ground. The snake then pulls its body up to the scales. This makes it slide forward in a straight line.

It seems as if it would be hard to move without legs. But snakes do it well.

A sidewinder crawls by jumping
along the ground, sideways.

Sidewinder Rattlesnake

Playing hide and seek with the sun

It is night in a desert. A small lizard lies covered with sand. Only its head sticks out. It is using the sand like a blanket to keep its body warm during the cool night.

When the sun comes up, the lizard crawls out of the sand. It moves very slowly because it is cold. It lies on a rock for a long time, letting the sun warm it.

When its body is warm enough, the lizard dashes off to look for food.

Many times during the day, the lizard's body grows too hot in the bright sunshine. Then it crawls into the shade of a rock until its body cools off a little.

Fringed-Toed Iguanid

Lizards and all other reptiles are cold blooded. Their bodies get just as hot or cold as the air or water around them. If their bodies get cold, reptiles can't move well. And if their bodies get too hot, reptiles die. So reptiles must help their bodies by playing hide and seek with the sun. If they are cold, they lie in warm sunshine. If they are hot, they hurry into shade. Alligators, crocodiles, and turtles go into cool water when they are hot.

A reptile that lives where winters are cold moves more and more slowly as cold weather comes. The reptile curls up in the warmest hole it can find. Its body grows cold and stiff. It cannot move at all. Only when warm weather returns can the reptile move and start its life again.

98

It's an Amphibian

Did you ever see a big, fat frog? A frog is one of the animals that lives in water when it is a baby and on land when it grows up. We call these animals amphibians.

Amphibians lay eggs that are soft and have no shells. The eggs dry up easily, so amphibians must lay them in water or wet places. Most baby amphibians are born in water. They look like baby fish and breathe with gills as a fish does.

When amphibians grow up their gills disappear. Then the amphibians come on land to live. They breathe with lungs as birds, dogs, and people do.

The word *amphibian* means *two lives*. That's a good name for animals that live one kind of life in water and another kind of life on land.

The European green toad is an amphibian.

The spotted salamander is an amphibian.

The red-eyed tree frog is an amphibian. ▶

This amphibian

This is a looking page. It can show you many things about this frog, if you look carefully.

See the frog's big, round eyes? They are on the very top of its head. The frog can peek out of the water without having to stick its whole head above water. Do you think this helps the frog stay safer?

The frog's back legs look big and strong, don't they? Big, strong back legs are what make the frog such a wonderful jumper. And the frog does all its swimming with its back legs.

The feet on the frog's back legs are like big flippers. They help the frog swim.

The frog's front legs are smaller than its back legs. The frog rests its front feet on the ground when it sits. Sometimes it uses its front feet like hands, to push insects and other food into its mouth.

Look at the frog's skin. If you could touch it, do you think it would feel bumpy or smooth?

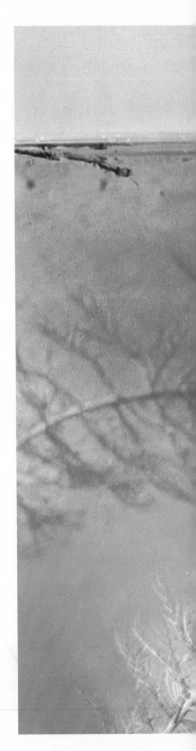

Water Frog

Green Frog and American Toad

Amphibians all

Frogs and toads look much alike. But toads are fatter than frogs and have shorter back legs. A toad's skin is rough and damp. A frog's skin is smooth and wet. Most toads have warts on their skin. But you won't catch warts if you touch a toad.

Newts

Red Salamander

Mud Puppy (Salamander)

Caecilian

Frogs and toads have no tails. The amphibians called salamanders and newts all have tails. There are many kinds of newts and salamanders. Pygmy salamanders, which live in the United States, are no longer than one of your fingers. Giant salamanders, which live in Japan, are longer than you are tall.

The strangest of all the amphibians are the caecilians. Caecilians live in tropical lands. They look like big, fat worms. Sometimes they are as big around as a man's thumb and as long as a yardstick.

Amphibians go hunting

Most kinds of amphibians hide and sleep during the day. At night they come creeping and hopping out to hunt for food.

Frogs and toads seem to be always hungry. And, in a way, they're a lot like lions and tigers because they hunt for live things to eat. Frogs and toads eat insects, worms, and even smaller frogs or toads. Big bullfrogs will even eat small turtles, snakes, mice, and birds.

Frogs and toads will eat only things that move. An insect or worm might be safe right in front of a frog or toad if it didn't move. But if it makes even the tiniest wiggle, the frog or toad will see it and gulp it down.

Many kinds of frogs and toads have long, sticky tongues that they use for catching food. If an insect comes near them, the frog or toad will slowly move closer —and closer. Then—*snap!* The tongue shoots out and pulls the insect into the amphibian's mouth.

Frogs and toads are skillful hunters. A scientist once watched a small toad catch 52 mosquitoes—in less than a minute!

Common Frog

The frog has caught a bush cricket.
It will use its front feet to push the
cricket down into its mouth.

The earthworm this toad caught was
longer than the toad. But the toad
will swallow it all down.

American Toad

Hiding from winter

Amphibians are cold-blooded. Their bodies are just about as warm or as cold as the air or water around them. So when winter comes, and the days get colder, an amphibian's body gets colder, too.

The amphibians try to get warm. Frogs and toads creep into deep holes that they find or dig. Many kinds of newts and salamanders crawl beneath logs, stones, or piles of leaves. Some salamanders and frogs dig into the bottom of the pond or river in which they live.

The weather turns colder. The frogs, toads, and salamanders huddle in their hiding places. Their bodies grow

Spotted Salamander in Winter

cold. They cannot move. Their breathing slows down and their hearts nearly stop beating. They must stay this way all through the cold days and nights of winter. And if their hiding places are not deep enough or warm enough, their bodies will grow so cold that they will die.

When spring comes along to warm up the world again, the amphibians begin to warm up, too. A few at a time they creep out of their hiding places. Then you begin to hear the *peep-peep* of the tree frogs and the *chuggerum* of the bullfrogs as the amphibians start their lives once more.

Spotted Salamander in Spring

The life of a grass frog

In early spring, the mother grass frog lays a thousand or more eggs in a lake or pond. Five days later, tiny wiggly tadpoles come out of the eggs.

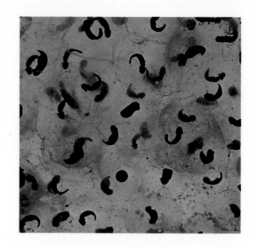

The tadpoles swim about, nibbling at plants. They breathe with gills, like fish. But lungs for breathing air are growing in their bodies.

After two months, the tadpoles grow little legs. A few weeks later they grow arms. Many tadpoles are eaten by fish and water insects.

After three months, the tadpoles can leave the water and breathe air with their lungs. They are now young frogs. Their short, tadpole tails will shrink away and vanish.

By summer's end, the frogs are full grown. During winter they will hibernate at the bottom of the pond. In the spring they will become fathers and mothers of new little tadpoles.

110

Many-Legged Creatures

Any sunny, summer day, in almost any back yard, empty lot, or lawn, you can see dozens of wild animals!

You're sure to see the eight-legged creature that catches other animals in a trap. It's a spider! And you may get to see the wonderful six-legged jumping animal that has its ears on its sides. It's a grasshopper! And if you find a ring of clay around a hole, it may be the front door of the ten-legged tunnel builder called a crayfish!

The world is full of these many-legged creatures. They are called arthropods. They live everywhere—jungles, deserts, oceans, caves, mountaintops, and in your back yard, where you can watch them creep, crawl, hop, dash, fly, hunt, fight, and eat, all summer long.

A crayfish is an arthropod.

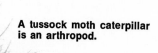

A tussock moth caterpillar is an arthropod.

A grasshopper is an arthropod. ▶

A ladybug is an arthropod.

Six legs

Did a fly ever land on your arm and tickle you? It was tickling with its six legs as it walked on your skin.

A fly is one of the six-legged animals we call insects. Flies, ants, bees, grasshoppers, beetles, crickets, and butterflies are all insects. They all have six legs.

All insects also have two wiggly feelers on their heads. And most kinds of insects have wings. Some, such as flies, have two wings. Some, such as dragonflies and beetles, have four wings.

Common Housefly

This is a grown-up fly. Baby flies can't fly. They have no wings. They look like tiny white caterpillars.

All insects have six legs and two feelers. Most insects have wings. And all insects' bodies are divided into three parts— head, chest, and stomach.

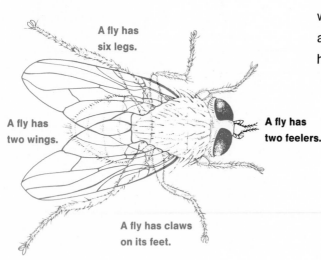

A fly has six legs.

A fly has two wings.

A fly has two feelers.

A fly has claws on its feet.

Insects are not at all like people. If you want to taste something, you put your tongue on it. But if a fly wants to taste something it walks on it! A fly tastes with its feet! When you want to smell something, you put your nose near it. But a fly has no nose. It smells things with the two feelers on its head. The fly can smell things better with its feelers than you can with your nose.

Insects don't see as we do either. An insect's eye is really hundreds of tiny eyes. Each tiny eye sees a piece of what the insect is looking at. This must make the insect see everything as though it were looking through a screen.

No matter where you live, some of these little six-legged animals are sure to be near you. There are nearly a million kinds of insects—and there are billions of each kind!

Long-Horned Milkweed Beetle

All insects have feelers. This beetle's feelers are quite long. Some insects have shorter ones.

Dragonfly

Some insects, such as this dragonfly, have four wings. Some insects have two wings.

Eight legs

Many people don't like spiders. But spiders help us. They eat many insects that are harmful to people.

Some spiders trap insects in webs made of silk. The silk comes out of tiny holes in the spider's body. The silk is a liquid that becomes a thin, strong thread when air touches it.

Different kinds of spiders make different kinds of webs. Garden spiders make sticky webs. Black widow spiders make tangled webs. Grass spiders make webs like little sheets.

Black Widow Spider

Some spiders hang nets of silk from corners or branches. Flying insects get tangled in the nets.

Some spiders dive into water and catch small fish and water insects.

Fisher Spider

Wolf spiders and lynx spiders catch insects by chasing them. Jumping spiders catch insects by jumping on them from several inches away.

Some spiders are fishermen. They wait by a stream or pond and catch water insects that swim past. Sometimes they dive into the water and grab fish. A raft spider makes a little boat of silk and leaves. When a small fish or water insect swims near the boat—the spider grabs it.

Spiders aren't insects. Insects have wings, feelers, and six legs. Spiders have no wings or feelers, and they have eight legs. Eight-legged animals are called arachnids.

Garden Spider

Some spiders fasten long, silk threads together like spokes of a wheel. They connect them with sticky threads on which insects get stuck. This kind of web is called an orb web.

An insect has six legs, wings, and feelers. But a spider has eight legs and no wings or feelers. A spider's skin is hard and covered with hair.

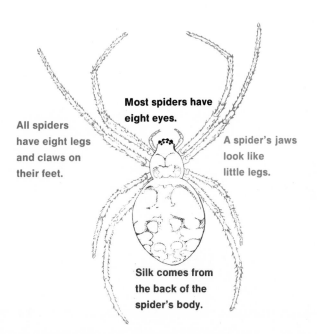

Most spiders have eight eyes.

All spiders have eight legs and claws on their feet.

A spider's jaws look like little legs.

Silk comes from the back of the spider's body.

Crab

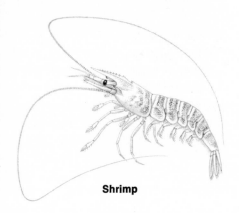
Shrimp

Barnacle

Ten legs

Creeping over the sandy sea bottom is an animal that looks like a big insect. But it has ten legs. Two of the legs have big claws. The animal has long feelers. Its body is covered with a hard shell. It's a lobster.

Lobsters, crabs, shrimps, and barnacles are *crustaceans*. That's a word that means *animal with a crust*. Every part of a lobster's body is covered with a crust of hard skin, like armor.

Crustaceans are cousins of the insects that fly and hop and creep about on land. But crustaceans are different from insects in several ways. Insects have six legs and two feelers. Crustaceans have at least ten legs, and four feelers. Insects breathe air through tiny holes in their bodies. Most crustaceans live in the water and breathe with gills, as fish do.

Crabs and lobsters look somewhat alike. But crabs have round, fat bodies. Lobsters have long bodies and wide, flat tails.

Shrimps are smaller than most crabs and lobsters. Some kinds of shrimps are so small they can be seen only with a microscope.

Barnacles are crustaceans that stop walking. When they are young they fasten themselves to rocks, floating pieces of wood, or the bottoms of ships. They are closed up inside their shells, with only their legs sticking out. They wiggle their legs to pull in tiny bits of food that float past in the water.

Lobster

Lobsters, crabs, shrimps, and barnacles are cousins of the insects that live on land.

A lobster walks with eight legs. It catches food with the claws on its other two legs. It swims by wiggling its tail. Its body is covered with a tough shell.

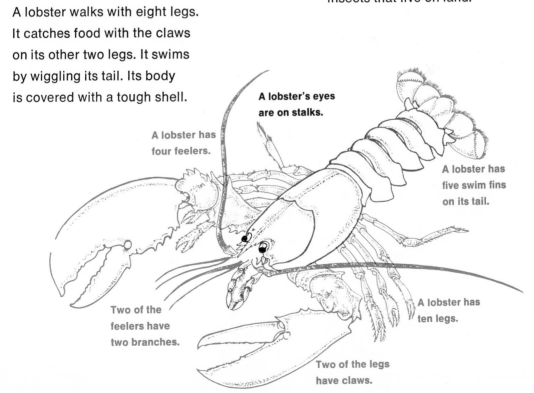

A lobster's eyes are on stalks.

A lobster has four feelers.

A lobster has five swim fins on its tail.

Two of the feelers have two branches.

A lobster has ten legs.

Two of the legs have claws.

Babies that hunt

Most baby insects start looking for food as soon as they leave their eggs. And the food for which some baby insects look is—other insects.

When a baby lacewing climbs out of its egg it goes hunting for aphids. Aphids are tiny insects that live on leaves. When the baby lacewing finds some aphids, it attacks them. It grabs an aphid and sucks its blood. Then it throws the dead aphid away and grabs another one. It kills every aphid in sight. Then it goes hunting for more. A baby lacewing is called a lion, because it is as fierce as a real lion.

A baby dragonfly is a fierce hunter, too. It lives in ponds and rivers and hunts water bugs, baby mosquitoes, and other water creatures. The baby dragonfly waits until something it can eat swims by. *Zip!* The baby dragonfly's lower lip shoots way out. On the end of the lip are two hooks. The hooks pinch together and catch the dragonfly's food. The lip snaps back and carries the food right into the baby dragonfly's mouth.

The insect called an ant lion is a baby, too. It is called an ant lion because it catches ants and eats them. The ant lion digs a cup-shaped hole in sand. It hides at the bottom of the hole with only its head sticking out. When an ant comes near the edge of the hole it slides down to the bottom of the hole. Then the ant lion has dinner.

This baby lacewing has caught its favorite food, an aphid. Baby lacewings are so fierce they are called lions.

Baby Lacewing Eating an Aphid

Baby dragonflies live in ponds and rivers. With the hooks on their long, lower lips, they catch other tiny water animals.

Baby Dragonfly Catching a Water Bug

An ant lion is a baby insect. It lives in a little pit in sand. When an ant falls into the pit, the ant lion eats it.

Ant Lion

A big change

A fat little brown and green caterpillar crawls on a leaf. A moth with beautiful black designs on its silver wings, flies past a bush. The moth and the caterpillar don't look a bit alike. But they are the same kind of animal. The caterpillar is a baby moth.

Every caterpillar you see in the summertime is a baby moth or butterfly. When a caterpillar comes out of its egg it spends a few weeks eating and growing. Then one day it's ready to change. Some caterpillars fasten themselves to tree trunks and cover themselves with silk that they make in their bodies. This silk covering is called a cocoon. Some caterpillars hang head down from tree branches. Their bodies become covered with hard shells. Some caterpillars dig into the ground.

Out of these little yellow balls will come tiny caterpillars. The caterpillars will eat and grow.

Puss Moth Eggs

A puss moth caterpillar looks like a twisted leaf. Its shape and color help it hide from enemies.

Puss Moth Caterpillar

The caterpillar goes to sleep in its cocoon, shell, or in the ground. Some caterpillars sleep during most of the summer and wake up in the fall. Some sleep during the winter and wake up in the spring. But when the caterpillar wakes from its long nap, it has changed.

It breaks out of its shell, or pushes out of its silk blanket, or crawls out of the ground. It isn't a short-legged caterpillar anymore. It has six long legs and two long feelers. Tiny raglike things on its back slowly swell up and become big wings. The crawling little caterpillar has become a flying creature—a moth or butterfly.

The caterpillar fastens itself to a twig. It covers itself with silk that it makes inside its body. It goes to sleep.

Puss Moth Cocoon

As it sleeps, the little caterpillar becomes a moth. It pushes out of the silk cocoon and flies away.

Puss Moth Adult

This grasshopper has grown too big for its baby skin. The skin dries and splits, and the grasshopper climbs out of it.

Changing skins

A young grasshopper climbs upon a twig. For a long time the grasshopper holds on to the twig without moving.

Then, a strange thing happens. The skin splits all along the grasshopper's back. Something pushes up out of the skin. It's the grasshopper. It is climbing out of its own skin!

All the many-legged creatures change skins many times during their lives. Insects, spiders, crabs, and lobsters all do it. For a few hours after changing skins, the new skins are soft. Then they turn hard like one of your fingernails.

In summer you may see what looks like a dead insect clinging to a twig or plant stem. It's an empty skin that an insect has grown out of and left behind.

The grasshopper's new wings are tiny and crumpled. As the grasshopper breathes the wings fill with blood and stretch out.

The soft, new skin will become hard in a few hours. When the grasshopper grows too big, it will change skins again.

Grasshopper

Chirp, creak, buzz

Zeet-zeet-zeet!
Cree-cree-cree!
Ch-ch-ch-ch-urrrrr!
Those are some of the insect noises you can hear on a hot summer night.

Most of the chirps, creaks, and buzzes you hear are made by crickets, grasshoppers, katydids, and cicadas. The male insects make some of these noises to call to the female insects.

None of these insects makes its noise with its mouth. A male katydid makes its noise by rubbing its wings together. On one wing the katydid has a row of little teeth. On the other wing is a hard little scraper. When the scraper is rubbed over the teeth it makes the noise. You can make the same kind of noise by rubbing a pencil over the teeth of a comb.

Most insects make a buzzing noise when they fly. The noise is made by their wings moving up and down. Even so small an insect as a housefly makes a loud buzzing when it flies. But no insect has a voice. And although insects seem able to hear, most of them have no ears.

Grasshoppers, crickets, and katydids have ears, though. But the ears are in strange places. A grass-hopper's ears are on its sides! And a katydid's ears are on its legs!

Katydid

This insect gets its name from the noise it makes. The noise sounds like "katy did-katy didn't-katy did-katy didn't."

This is what a katydid's noisemakers look like through a microscope. They are on the male katydid's wings.

This is what a female katydid's leg looks like through a microscope. The hole is her ear.

Honeybee

The bee's sting protects it.

Stinkbug

A bad smell protects this bug.

This insect's shape protects it.

Walking Stick

Protection for insects

Insects are always in danger from many other animals. But many insects have ways of protecting themselves.

Many insects can fight back if they are attacked. Wasps, bees, hornets, and some other insects can give painful stings. Stinkbugs chase other insects away by spraying bad smells at them. The bombardier beetle shoots out a stinging, bad-tasting spray that will even chase frogs away.

Some insects are good at pretending to be something else. They don't do this on purpose, of course—they're just made that way. But when a katydid sits on a branch it looks like a leaf. Many kinds of moths look like pieces of tree bark. And walking sticks and some moth caterpillars look like twigs. Looking like something else is a good way for these insects to hide from other animals that might eat them.

Ladybugs, monarch butterflies, and some other insects taste bad. These insects are always brightly colored, orange and black. These colors say, "I taste bad!" Birds learn not to eat these insects. The insects are protected by their color.

Monarch Butterfly

Viceroy Butterfly

Monarch butterflies taste bad to birds. Birds learn to tell monarch butterflies by their bright colors, and leave them alone. Viceroy butterflies don't taste bad. But they look much like monarch butterflies, so birds leave them alone, too. Both butterflies are protected by their bright colors.

But some insects that don't taste bad are colored orange and black, too. Birds are fooled by their colors and leave them alone. So those insects are protected by their colors, too.

Many-legged home builders

In the sandy ground at the edge of a desert there is a small, round hole. Fastened to the hole is a little, round door. The door is open. What lives in this strange little house?

The hole in the sand is the doorway of a trap-door spider's home. The spider makes a long tunnel and lines it with silk. It

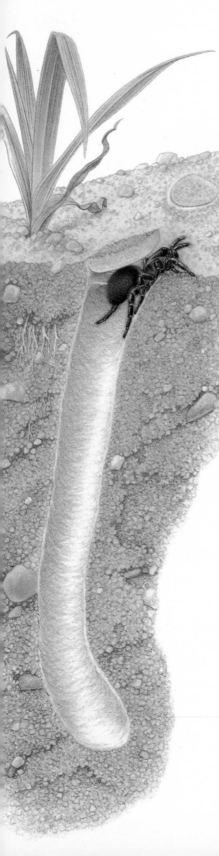

A trap-door spider's home is a silk-lined tunnel with a door made of silk and dirt.

Trap-Door Spider

Harvester ants live in tunnels that they dig in the ground.

Harvester Ants

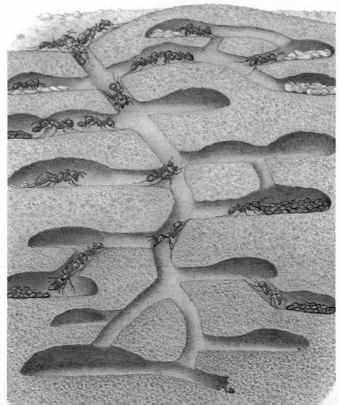

makes a door of silk mixed with dirt. There is even a sort of little handle on the inside of the door. The spider can hold the door shut from the inside if an enemy tries to get in.

Lots of other many-legged animals make homes for themselves, too. The homes are made of silk, leaves, sand, dirt, and wood.

The purse web spider makes a long silk tube next to a tree trunk. The spider spends its whole life inside its long, round home.

The insect called a leaf roller makes itself a new house every day. It pulls a leaf around itself and fastens the edges together with silk that it makes in its body. Then it eats the inside of its house!

Many kinds of ants build whole cities. They dig tunnels and storerooms in dirt, sand, or wood. In some of the rooms they keep food, and in others they keep the queen ant's eggs.

One kind of termite makes a nest of dirt mixed with glue that comes from its body. The nests are taller than a man and harder than rock!

Valley Carpenter Bee

The bee makes rooms inside a hollow stem. In each room is a white baby bee and a yellow ball of honey.

Paper Wasp

Some wasp nests are made of paper tubes. The wasps make the paper by chewing wood.

The World of the Sea

Imagine an animal that has ten eyes, ten arms that shoot poison, and a body made of jelly! There really is such an animal. It's called a jellyfish and it lives in the sea.

The sea is filled with animals. It's the home of the frogfish and the eight-armed octopus. It's the home of the flying fish and the conch—a giant snail with a claw and a huge, twisted shell.

The sea is the home of animals that swim and float and creep, and of animals that fasten themselves down and never move again. It is the home of some of the tiniest of all animals and of the biggest animal that has ever lived.

The sea is a beautiful place. And it's a frightening place. It's a wonderland and a fairyland. It's another world!

The flying fish lives in the sea.

The conch lives in the sea.

The octopus lives in the sea.

The frogfish lives in the sea. ▶

Sea animals

The sea is filled with many kinds of animals. Fish, crabs, oysters, snails, and most other sea animals stay under water all the time. But whales, dolphins, sea turtles, sea snakes, and others breathe air. They must put their heads above water to breathe.

Many sea animals don't look like the kind of animal they really are. The eel looks like a snake, but it's a fish. Dolphins and whales look like fish, but they're not. They are mammals, like seals and walruses. And sponges, sea anemones, and corals don't even look like animals. They look like plants.

Northern Fur Seal

Jellyfish

Sperm Whale

Pacific Walrus

Bottle-Nosed Dolphin

Sardines

Elephant-Ear Sponge

Green Moray Eel

Green Crab

Pearl Oyster

Moon Snail

Danger—shut the lid!

An oyster is an animal that spends nearly all its life lying in a box!

An oyster moves about only while it is a baby. A baby oyster is a round little lump, no bigger than the head of a pin. It swims by wiggling tiny hairs on its body. It's as soft as a gumdrop, but when it's a day old it begins to grow a hard shell. In about a week, the shell covers the oyster's whole body. A week later the oyster fastens itself to a rock and never moves again.

The oyster's shell is really two shells. They are held together by a hinge that's part of the oyster's body. The oyster lies in the bottom shell and, most of the time, holds the top shell open, like a lid. That's how the oyster spends its whole life. It's like living in a box.

The oyster has to keep its shell open so it can eat. It eats tiny plants and animals in the water that flows past its body. When its shell is open, the oyster is in danger. Lots of animals like to eat oysters.

But an oyster can quickly close its shell when danger is near. The oyster has no eyes, ears, or nose, but it has many tiny feelers. The feelers can tell when something is coming near the oyster. Then—*snap!* Down comes the lid!

An oyster can close its shell so tightly that not even a big, strong man can pull it apart. Some animals have ways of opening an oyster's shell. But when an oyster closes its lid, it's safe from most of the hungry animals that live in the world of the sea.

Oyster

An oyster's shell is like a box with a lid. The oyster lies inside the box and holds the lid open, as the oyster in the top picture is doing. In the bottom picture an oyster's shell has been opened all the way. You can see the soft, gray, lumpy oyster lying in its shell.

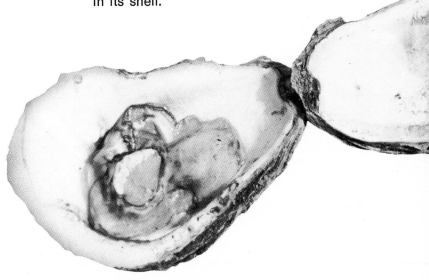

Living in a cup

An animal like a tiny flower floats down through the water of the sea. It fastens itself to the sandy bottom. It takes minerals out of the water and builds a tiny stone cup around itself.

After a while the little animal buds, just as a flower does. The bud grows and becomes another flower animal. The new animal builds a stone cup around itself. Then the new animal buds, too.

After many years, there is a big pile of the tiny stone cups, all stuck together. Inside each cup is one of the little flowerlike animals. During the day, each little animal hides inside its cup. At night, each animal stretches

Thousands of tiny animals that look like little flowers live in this lacy-looking coral.

Lace Coral

its body and holds out arms that look like flower petals. The arms catch tiny animals that swim near.

The stone cups stuck together are called coral. When a little flowerlike animal is inside each cup the coral looks like a field of flowers. The little animals are colored, so the coral may be red, pink, orange, blue, green, or purple. And different kinds of flowerlike animals put their cups together in different ways. The coral may be shaped like a bush, a fan, a round ball, or a bunch of lace.

Live coral is beautiful to see. It makes the world of the sea look like a fairyland.

Star Coral by Day

During the day, all the tiny coral animals are hiding inside their cups.

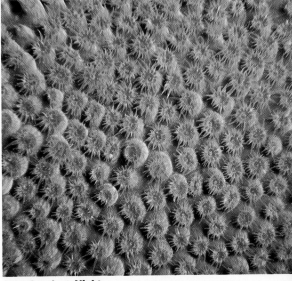

Star Coral at Night

At night, the coral animals come partway out. They spread their many arms to catch food.

Sun Starfish

A starfish's points are its arms. Most starfish have five arms. Some have many more.

Growing a new arm

There's an animal that has eyes and feet on its arms and turns its stomach inside out when it eats! And if it loses an arm—it grows a new one!

The animal is a starfish. Its body is shaped like a star. Each of the points of the star is an arm. Most starfish have five arms, but some have as many as fifty arms. On the underside of each arm are many tiny tubes. These are the starfish's feet. At the tip of each arm is a bunch of little spots. These are the starfish's eyes. They

A starfish's feet are on the bottoms of its arms. The feet look like tiny tubes.

Common Starfish

can only see light and dark.

If a starfish has an arm bitten or torn off by another animal, the starfish can grow a new one. Sometimes an arm that has been torn off can grow a whole new starfish!

When a starfish finds a clam, oyster, or scallop it climbs onto it. The starfish pulls at each half of the clam or oyster shell. It pushes its stomach out through its mouth and slides it between the two halves of the shell. And it digests the clam or oyster right inside its own shell.

A starfish pulls a clam's shell apart.
Then the starfish puts its stomach
into the shell and digests the clam.

Starfish and Clam

The pasture of the sea

Billions and billions of tiny plants and animals live in the ocean. Most of them are so small they can be seen only with a microscope.

These tiny plants aren't like plants you have seen. Some look like squares of jelly fastened together in chains. Some look like little balls. Some are like tiny anchors with threads hanging from them.

The tiny animals are strange looking, too. Some look like bells. Some look like light bulbs with six wiggly legs. Some of them are just little round balls. Many of these animals are the babies of bigger animals, such as jellyfish.

All these plants and animals float in the upper part of the ocean. They are called plankton. Plankton is the most important food in the sea. It is often called the pasture of the sea.

Many kinds of baby fish eat plankton. So do many grown fish. So do many other sea animals. If suddenly there were no plankton, all these animals would die. And all the animals that eat them for food would then die. Soon there wouldn't be a single living thing in any of the oceans.

That's why plankton is the most important food in the sea.

Billions of tiny plants and animals float in the ocean. They are called plankton. They are the food of many of the big animals in the ocean. This is what plankton looks like through a microscope.

Plankton

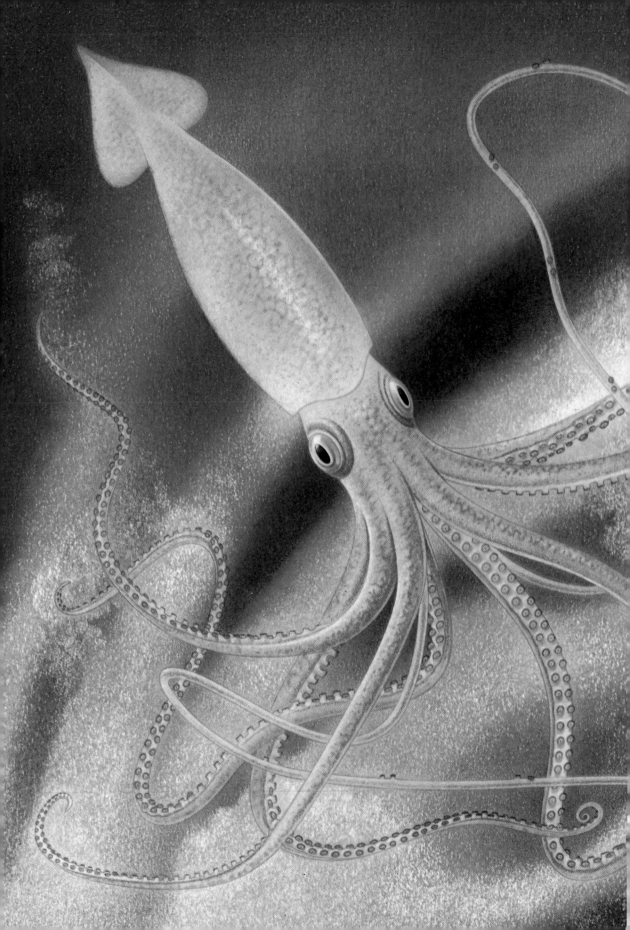

A real sea monster

Long ago, people believed in sea monsters. One of the monsters was called the kraken. People said it had ten arms and was so big it could swallow a whole ship.

Today, we know there is no such thing as a kraken. But there really are animals somewhat like it. They live deep in the ocean. They are giant squids.

A squid has eight, long, pointed, wiggly arms and two other arms like long paddles. The squid's eyes are wide and staring. It's body is inside a shell that has a shape somewhat like an ice cream cone.

Most squids aren't much longer than a man's hand. But giant squids are longer than two school buses in a row. Their eyes are as big as dinner plates. Giant squids are real sea monsters!

Giant squids are the favorite food of big sperm whales. The whales dive into the deep, dark parts of the ocean where the squids live. There are terrible battles when a big whale meets a giant squid. The squid wraps its long arms around the whale and squeezes. Most of the time the whale wins the fight and eats the squid. Many whales have been seen with marks of a giant squid's arms on their bodies.

Giant Squid

Biggest of all!

What is the biggest animal that has ever lived?

It's not one of the giant dinosaurs of long ago. It's an animal that is living right now. It is the blue whale.

A blue whale is so long and wide that eight elephants in a row could stand on its back!

Whales look like big fish. But whales aren't fish. They are mammals. They spend all their lives in water, but they breathe air, just as we do. If a whale stays under-water too long, it drowns.

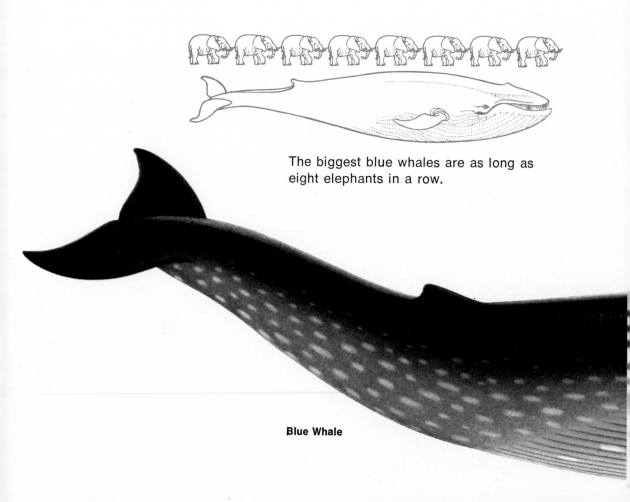

The biggest blue whales are as long as eight elephants in a row.

Blue Whale

It seems as if big whales should eat big things. But most whales' throats are too small to swallow anything bigger than an orange! So the biggest of all animals eat the smallest things in the ocean. Blue whales, right whales, bowheads, and finbacks eat plankton. Plankton is made up of plants and animals so tiny you can't see them without a microscope.

Other whales are meat-eaters. Narwhals and bottlenoses eat fish, crabs, and lobsters. Sperm whales eat fish, too. But a sperm whale's favorite food is giant squid. Killer whales eat seals and porpoises. Killer whales attack men, too.

Once, there were many whales in the seas. But men have hunted whales for many years. The whales are killed for meat and oil. Now there aren't many whales left. The big blue whales have almost all been killed. The biggest animal that ever lived may soon be gone forever.

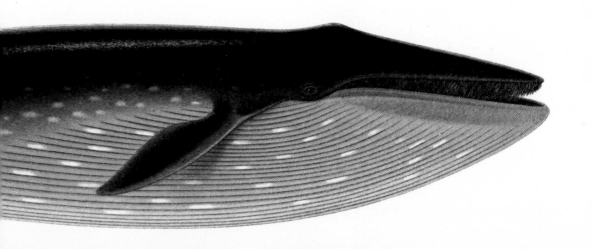

Sea Peaches

The sea peach is one kind of sea squirt. Sea squirts suck water in, then squirt it out.

To eat, a sea cucumber slides its arms through the sand or mud, puts them into its mouth and sucks the mud off them!

Sea Cucumber

Sea peaches, cucumbers, grapes

You would never find a sea peach in a basket of fruit, or a sea cucumber in a salad. Because a sea peach isn't a fruit and a sea cucumber isn't a vegetable. They're animals!

Sea peaches belong to the family of animals called sea squirts. Most kinds of sea squirts are just round bodies with two openings like little mouths. One mouth sucks water in. The other mouth squirts water out. The sea squirt eats the tiny animals and bits of plants in the water it sucks in.

Sea squirts stay fastened to the rocks or sand and never move. But sea cucumbers crawl slowly over the sand and mud. They crawl on many feet that look like little tubes.

A sea cucumber has a long, round body with what looks like a bunch of leaves at one end. These are the sea cucumber's "fingers." It eats by sucking food off them just as you might lick jelly from your fingers. As the sea cucumber crawls, it rubs its "fingers" in the sand or mud. Bits of food stick to them. Then the sea cucumber puts them in its mouth, one at a time, and cleans them.

The sea peach and sea cucumber aren't the only sea animals that look like other things. The sea urchin looks like a round pincushion with pins sticking out all over it. The sea grape is a little sea squirt that looks like a green grape. And the sand dollar is an animal that looks like a cooky!

Sea Urchin

A sea urchin's round body is covered with spikes. Some sea urchins' spikes are poisonous.

This looks like a cooky, but it's a sea animal that moves about on many feet that look like tiny tubes.

Sand Dollar

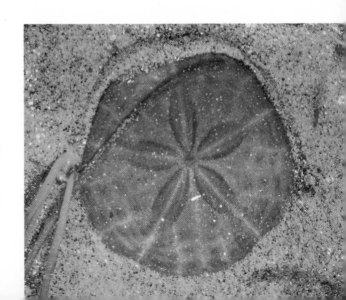

The Hidden World

A vorticella is so small you can't see it without a microscope.

This very minute, all around you, billions and billions of living things are crawling and creeping and floating. But you can't see any of them! They're so tiny they are hidden from your eyes. They are so tiny that thousands of them can live in one drop of water this small ◊ .

You can see these little living things only with a microscope. These tiny creatures don't look anything like dogs or frogs or any of the animals you know about. These tiny creatures look like drops of jelly or like slippers, barrels, and ice cream cones made of glass.

Most creatures that live in the hidden world are called protists. They are small and strange-looking, but they move and hunt and eat just as big animals do. Tiny protists are as much a part of the great, living world as an elephant or a whale.

A paramecium is so small you can't see it without a microscope.

A euglena is so small you can't see it without ▶ a microscope.

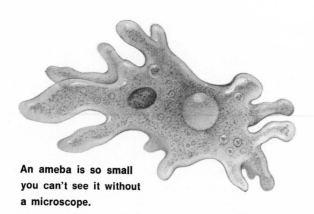

An ameba is so small you can't see it without a microscope.

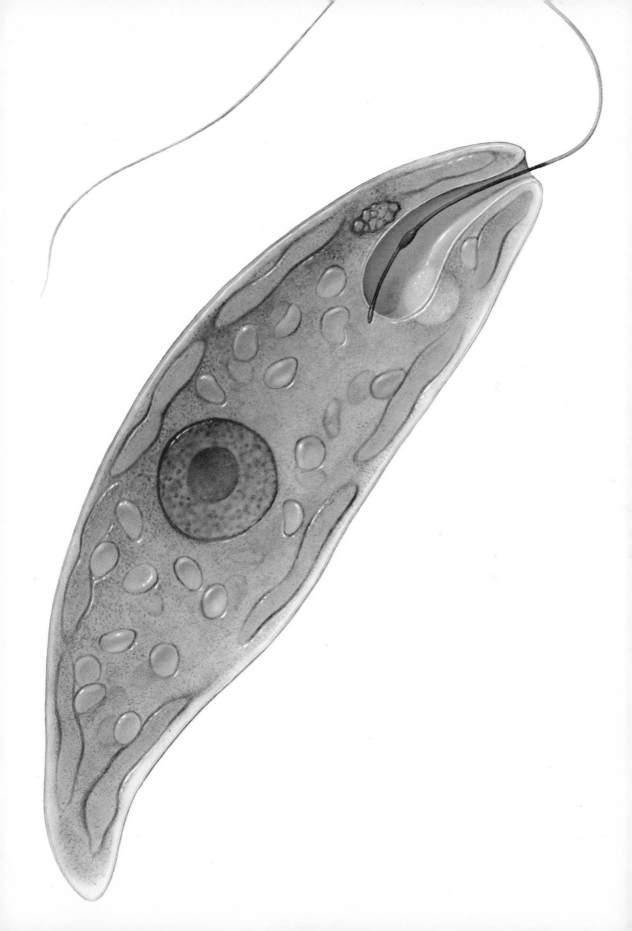

Seeing the invisible

If you spread some jelly on bread and the jelly suddenly crawled away, you'd think you were seeing things. But sometimes, in the woods after a rain, you can see what looks like jelly crawling on wet logs or stumps!

Most creatures of the hidden world can't be seen without a microscope. But sometimes thousands or even millions of them will come together in a crowd, and the crowd can be seen. That's what this strange, crawling jellylike stuff is—a huge crowd of tiny, living creatures all fastened together. It's called a slime mold.

The slime mold is usually about as big as a man's hand. It crawls slowly over wet logs, leaves, and stumps. It eats tiny creatures of the hidden world and bits of plants. After a while it stops moving and begins to dry up. It changes into many little balls or rods. Inside these are powdery seedlike things called spores.

The balls or rods burst open and the spores fly out. If a spore lands where there is water, the spore becomes a tiny creature, too small to be seen except with a microscope.

After a time, the tiny creature splits into two new creatures that stay fastened together. The pair of creatures joins other pairs, and soon a new jellylike slime mold, made up of thousands of tiny creatures, is slowly creeping along. Slime molds move, as animals do, but they come from a sort of seed, as plants do. Like many hidden world creatures, they seem to be both plants and animals at the same time!

This may look like jelly crawling on a log. But it's really many tiny living creatures, all fastened together.

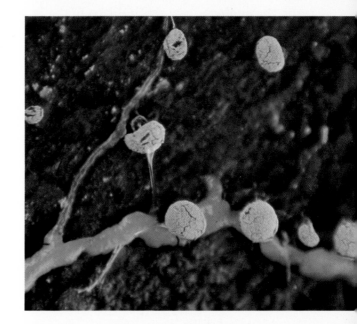

The jellylike stuff stops moving. It changes into many tiny balls. Inside the balls are seedlike things called spores.

The balls pop open. A cloud of spores shoots into the air. From the spores will come tiny creatures that will multiply and fasten together to make new jellylike slime molds.

Slime Mold

What are they?

Are the tiny creatures of the hidden world animals or plants? Sometimes they seem to be one thing, and sometimes they seem to be another.

The creature called a euglena lives in ponds and water-filled ditches. A euglena is usually green, like a plant. And in sunlight the euglena uses the light to make its own food, just as a plant does. So some scientists say the euglena is a plant.

But a euglena moves around as an animal does. And when a euglena is in darkness it loses its green color. It hunts for its food as an animal does. So some scientists say that euglena is really an animal.

But other scientists say that it isn't right to call euglena either a plant *or* an animal. They say that euglena needs a different name to show that it is different from both plants and animals. They know that creatures like euglena were some of the first living things on earth. So they call euglena a *protist*, which means *the very first*.

Many scientists call all the tiny creatures of the hidden world protists.

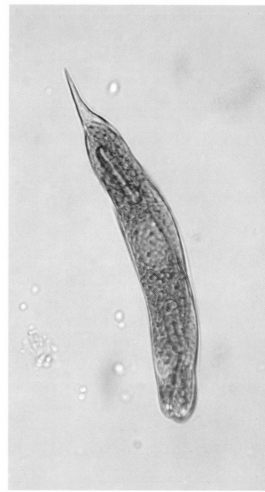

Euglena

This creature, like many creatures in the hidden world, seems like a plant sometimes and like an animal at other times. Some scientists have named all these tiny creatures protists.

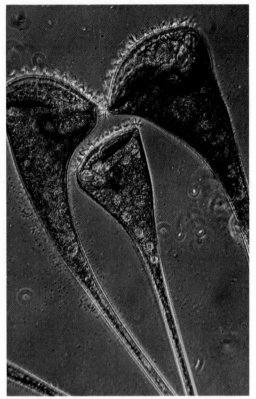

Stentors

These are some of the biggest
of all protists. They eat by
sucking smaller creatures
into their hornlike "mouths."

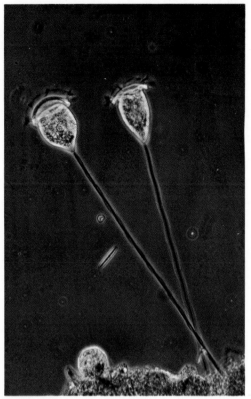

Vorticellae

These protists look like
flowers on stems. But they
are more like animals than
like plants.

This creature has rows of
tiny hairs on its body.
It swims by using the
hairs as paddles.

Paramecium

This protist creeps along
by using its bunches of
tiny hairs like little legs.

Euplotes

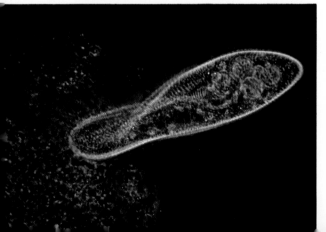

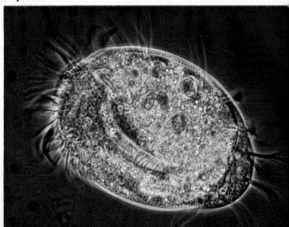

An ocean in a teaspoon

Pretend that you have microscope eyes. You're going to look at a teaspoonful of water from a pond.

The water looks clear to everyone else. But with microscope eyes you can see that there are hundreds of thousands of tiny creatures swimming in the water. A teaspoonful of water is like an ocean to the tiny creatures of the hidden world.

They are strange-looking creatures. One of them looks like a glass slipper. It has no head or legs or eyes or mouth. Its body is covered with rows of little hairs. It uses these hairs like little oars to move itself through the water. This creature is called a paramecium.

Suddenly, another creature appears. It looks like a piece of gray jelly with bubbles in it. It changes shape every time it moves. It moves by pushing part of itself forward like a long arm. Then it uses the arm to pull the rest of itself forward. This creature is an ameba.

The ameba moves toward the paramecium. It sends long curling arms over and under and around the paramecium. The paramecium is trapped! Suddenly it is inside the ameba! The paramecium will slowly fade away as the ameba digests it.

Many different kinds of tiny creatures, called protists, can be found in a teaspoonful of pond water. They are some of the smallest of all living things.

Through a microscope the
creature called an ameba looks
like a moving drop of jelly.
As it creeps along it bumps
into a smaller creature called
a paramecium.

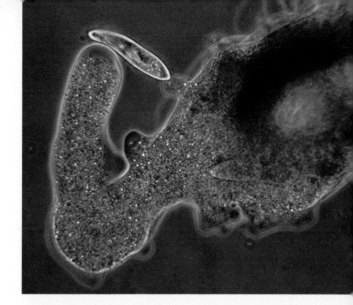

The ameba pulls the
paramecium in toward itself.
Its whole body begins to move
around the paramecium.

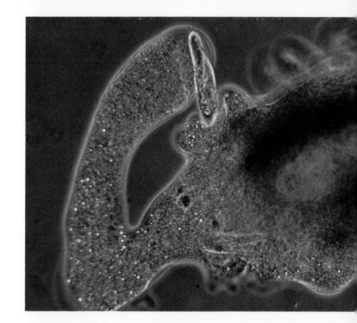

Now the paramecium is inside
the ameba. It has become food.
It will slowly fade away as
the ameba digests it.

Ameba and Paramecium

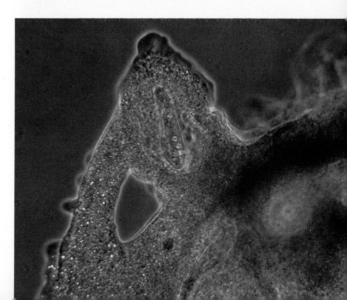

Bigger eats smaller

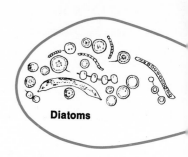

Diatoms

Do you know you're part of a food chain?

The food chain begins in the hidden world. Billions and billions and billions of tiny plants called diatoms float in the ocean. You would need a strong microscope to see them. Like most plants, they make their own food, using sunlight.

Living in the ocean with the diatoms are billions of tiny shrimplike animals called copepods. They are much bigger than diatoms. But you would still need a microscope to see them. And each copepod eats more than a hundred thousand diatoms every day.

Swimming about among the diatoms and copepods are little fish called herring. They're only about 12 inches long but they're giants next to the copepods. Each herring eats thousands of copepods.

And the herrings are gobbled up by bigger fish such as the cod. Full grown codfish are about 3 feet long.

Codfish are very important food fish for people. Fishermen in ships catch codfish in big nets. The codfish are cleaned and cut into pieces. The pieces are frozen and sent to grocery stores.

Your mother buys some of the frozen fish pieces at the store. She brings the fish home and cooks it for dinner. When you eat the fish, the food chain that started with the tiny diatoms of the hidden world reaches you.

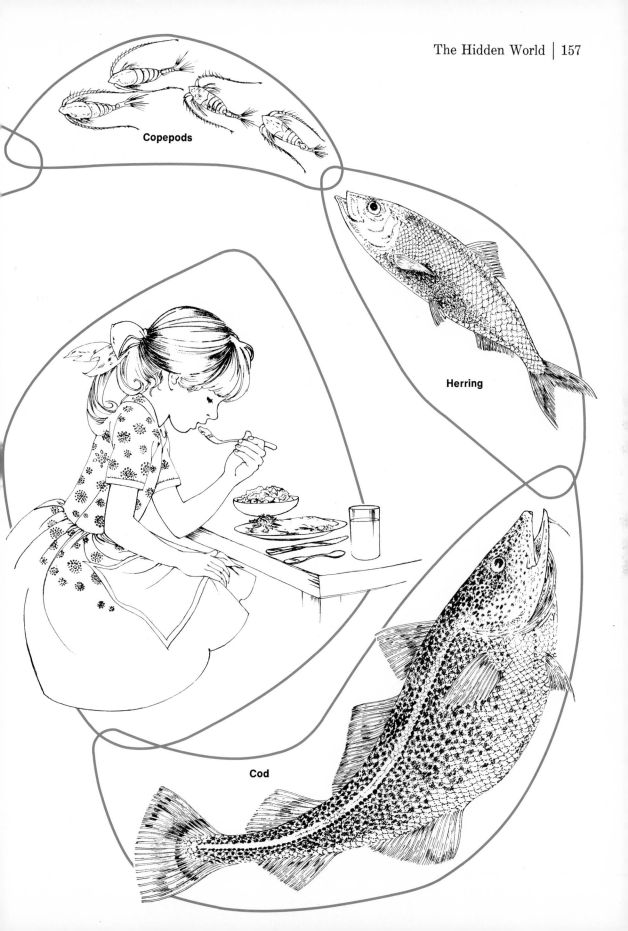

Copepods

Herring

Cod

Staying Alive

A tawny frogmouth's color and shape help it stay alive.

Far up near the North Pole a tiny, baby seal lies in the snow. If a polar bear saw the baby seal, the bear would eat it up in a minute!

But the polar bear cannot see the baby seal. The seal's stiff, white fur is the same color as the snow. The baby seal is protected by its color.

Most animals need some kind of protection to keep from being eaten. Some animals are protected by their shape or color, like the baby seal. Some animals are protected by armor. Some are good fighters. Some are fast runners.

But whether it runs or fights or hides, nearly every animal must have some way of protecting itself—to stay alive!

A porcupine's quills help it stay alive.

A seal pup's color helps it stay alive. ▶

A gazelle's speed help it stay alive.

Hiding with color

Hop! A green grasshopper shoots up out of the grass. It sails through the air and lands in the grass again. You can't see it before it jumps. And you can't see it after it comes down. Its green color helps it hide in the green grass.

An animal is hard to see if it is the same color as the ground, rocks, or plants around it. A green caterpillar on a green leaf is hard to see, and so is a brown horned toad on brown sand. The caterpillar's color helps it hide from birds while it is eating. The horned toad's color helps it hide from birds and snakes while it looks for insects to eat.

The spots and stripes that many animals have on their bodies help them hide, too. A giraffe's body is pale orange or white, with reddish-brown spots. When the giraffe walks among trees it seems to disappear. Its spotted body looks like spots of sunlight and shadow among the leaves.

A tiger's coat is orange-brown with black stripes. When the tiger lies in a field of brown grass striped with sun and shadow, it can't be seen. When another animal comes near enough, the tiger can jump out of hiding at it.

The color and designs on an animal's body help it hide so it can get food—or so it can keep from becoming food!

Giraffe

The colors and designs on a giraffe's body help the giraffe hide when it stands among the trees.

Tomato Hornworm

A hungry bird may not be able to see a green caterpillar on a green leaf.

Pheasant

The colors of a pheasant's feathers make it look like a pile of leaves.

Changing color

How would you like to play hide-and-seek with a chameleon?

You'd have a hard time finding this tiny lizard. It can hide by changing color! It can be green on a green leaf, yellow on yellow sand, and gray on a gray rock.

The kind of shrimp called a prawn is an even better color changer than a chameleon. The prawn can be green when it swims among green seaweed, orange when it is near orange coral, and brown on brown rocks. At night, when the water is dark blue, the prawn turns blue, too.

A champion color changer is the fish called a sole. It can turn yellow, brown, blue, green, and even pink. It can even turn more than one color at a time. If it lies on brown sand that has little yellow stones in it, the sole's body turns brown with yellow spots! Scientists once put a sole into a tank that had a polka dot design on the bottom. The sole's body turned polka-dotted!

How do these animals change color? Under the animal's skin are many tiny, tiny sacs filled with color. Tubes like little tree branches reach up from the sacs to the skin. Different kinds of light on the animal's skin make the tubes fill up with color, and this colors the skin.

An animal that can change color is lucky. It can stay hidden wherever it goes.

Sole

These pictures show how a sole
changes color to match the
bottom over which it swims.
In the last picture, the sole
has matched the color of the
sand so well that you can
hardly see it.

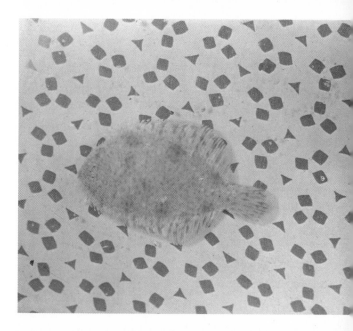

Sole

Sole

Animal actors

Many animals protect themselves by pretending.

The frilled lizard is small and harmless. But it pretends to be big and dangerous. When it opens its mouth its throat is bright red and frightening. A big flap of skin on its neck lifts up and spreads out. The lizard suddenly looks much bigger and very dangerous!

The harmless hog-nosed snake pretends to be dangerous, too. It opens its mouth and hisses. It pretends it's going to bite. But then, if its enemy isn't frightened, the hog-nosed snake acts dead. It rolls over onto its back and lies still. Most animals don't care to eat dead snakes, so the enemy usually goes away.

Some animals pretend that they aren't even animals. The bird called a tawny frogmouth pretends to be part of a tree. Its feathers look like bark. It sits on a branch, stretches itself out, and closes its eyes. It looks just like a broken branch.

Some animal actors have disguises that protect them from enemies and help them get food at the same time. The South American leaf fish looks just like a leaf floating in the water. Bigger fish pass right by it. But when a smaller fish swims near—*gulp!* The leaf fish swallows it down!

These animal actors don't know they're pretending. It's just one of the ways they stay alive.

Frilled Lizard

When this lizard is in danger, it opens its mouth. Then the big piece of skin around its neck lifts up.

With the piece of skin stretched out, the lizard looks much bigger to other animals. They are frightened away.

This snake isn't really dead. It's only acting. This is how the snake protects itself from animals that might eat it.

Hog-Nosed Snake

Pangolin

Animals in armor

If you saw a pangolin you might say it looked like a pine cone with legs and a tail.

A pangolin is one of the animals that is protected by armor. It's covered with scales like the scales on a pine cone, only bigger. When a pangolin is frightened it rolls itself into a ball. It tucks its head between its legs and covers its stomach with its tail. Its sharp-edged scales stick up. Not even a tiger would care to try to bite through them.

The armadillo is another animal in armor. In fact, the word *armadillo* means *little armored thing*. Armadillos are born with soft skin. But as they grow, their skins become covered with small, flat pieces of bone. This bony armor covers an armadillo's back, sides, head, tail, and the insides of its legs. The armadillo protects itself by rolling into a ball as the pangolin does. Then it's a hard, bony ball that a wolf or bobcat finds hard to bite.

Porcupines, hedgehogs, porcupine fish, and sea urchins wear a sort of armor, too. Their bodies are covered with sharp stickers that keep other animals from biting them.

Pangolins, armadillos, porcupines, hedgehogs, and sea urchins can't run fast, hide, or fight well. Wearing armor helps them stay alive.

Nine-Banded Armadillo

Armadillos can't fight well. They need their armor to protect them from animals that might eat them.

When an armadillo is in danger it rolls itself into a ball. Every part of its body is protected by the tough armor.

Lion and Wildebeests

A race for life

When you run in a race, it's just for fun. But many kinds of animals run in races that often mean life or death for one of them.

When a lion hunts a wildebeest it tries to creep as close as it can. If the lion gets close enough, it can jump on the wildebeest's back and kill it. But if the wildebeest sees or smells the lion, it dashes away. Then the race begins!

Both animals run for their lives. The lion must catch the wildebeest so it can eat. The wildebeest must escape so it can go on living. If the wildebeest gets a quick start, or if the lion is old and slow, the wildebeest may get away. But if the lion is young and fast it will probably catch the wildebeest and kill it.

Animals that get their food by chasing other animals are fast runners. A man could never win a race against them. Foxes and wolves can run twice as fast as a man. A cheetah can run three times as fast as man. It's the fastest of all animals.

The kinds of animals that lions, wolves, and other hunting animals eat are fast runners, too. Gazelles can run faster than race horses. Jack rabbits and zebras are nearly as fast as gazelles. Even big, clumsy looking giraffes can run much faster than a man.

Lions, leopards, and cheetahs chase antelopes, wildebeests, and zebras. Wolves chase deer and elk. Coyotes and foxes chase rabbits. The hunter runs so it can eat. The animal it chases runs to keep from being eaten. The animal that wins the race is the one that stays alive!

Tooth and claw

The sun is setting on the cactus and sagebrush of a desert in North America. A badger is busily digging beside a bush.

Along comes a coyote. It sees the badger and licks its lips with a long, pink tongue. The coyote is planning to have a badger supper.

The badger tries to run. But the coyote dashes toward it and heads it off. The badger is trapped.

But suddenly the badger snarls, showing its sharp teeth! It rushes at the coyote and strikes at it with sharp claws!

The coyote jumps back. It is much bigger than the badger, but it doesn't like the looks of the badger's teeth and claws. The coyote trots off to find an easier supper. The badger has saved its life by fighting back.

The badger is a good fighter. But even animals that seem harmless will often fight to keep from being eaten. Zebras, giraffes, and deer kick with their hard, sharp hoofs. They can make deep, terrible cuts on an enemy. The harmless-looking ostrich defends itself by kicking, too. A kick from one of its big feet can break a hyena's back! When the giant anteater is in danger it stands up on its back legs and fights with the sharp claws on its front legs.

An animal uses whatever weapons it has when it is fighting for its life.

Coyote and Badger

The coyote would like to eat the badger,
but it's afraid. The badger is a good
fighter and will defend itself.

Animal Ways

A chaffinch's song
can be a warning.

Why do birds sing? Why do ants rush about so busily? Why does a mandrill sometimes seem to yawn when it sees another animal? Are there reasons for what the animals do?

Animals cannot think as people can. But there is nearly always a reason for the things animals do. A bird's song may be a warning of danger, a threat, or an invitation to a mate. Ants rush about to find food they can bring back to the nest. And the mandrill isn't yawning—he's warning the other animal not to come near or he'll fight!

Animals do things to protect themselves, to find food, or to be more comfortable. And sometimes they even do things just for fun.

Sometimes a mandrill's
yawn means "Keep away!" ▶

A harvester ant goes
to work every day.

African Elephants

A mother elephant protects her baby
by keeping it between her legs.
If the mother sees an enemy, she lifts
her trunk and makes a warning noise.

Protecting the babies

Snow whirls through the air. The wind howls. There's a blizzard coming to the icy land around the South Pole. That's where the emperor penguins live. The grown-up penguins hurry about, pushing all the baby penguins together. Then the grown-ups crowd together in a tight circle around the babies. This is how the grown-up penguins protect the babies from a storm.

In Africa, a mother elephant and her baby trot across a hot, grassy plain. The mother keeps the baby between her legs as she walks. This is how she protects it from animals that might try to kill it. If the mother sees an animal that might be an enemy, she raises her trunk. She makes a loud screaming noise. This warns the animal not to come too close!

Three brand-new baby herons lie in a nest in North America. The mother heron stands on the nest and fans the babies with her wings. The babies will die if they get too hot, so the mother heron keeps them cool.

Baby animals are in danger from many things. Many of them would die or be killed if they weren't protected. But many kinds of grown-up animals protect their babies from all the things that might harm them.

Sounds that say things

Red-Winged Blackbird

When a male bird sings in the springtime he is often telling other male birds to stay away.

Owls hoot. Foxes yap. Crickets chirp. Geese honk. Chipmunks chatter. And many of these animal sounds mean something.

Some animal noises are warnings. In the spring a male red-winged blackbird sings, *"Cock-a-ree!"* This is a warning to other male blackbirds. It means, "This is my place! Stay away or I'll fight you!"

Some animal noises are invitations. The tiny frogs called spring peepers make a noise that sounds like sleigh bells. The noise is made by male frogs to invite female frogs to come to them.

Some sounds are calls for help. A dolphin that is hurt or in trouble makes a high, whistling noise. Then other dolphins come to help it.

Some sounds mean "Danger!" If the bird called a chaffinch sees a hawk in the sky the chaffinch sings, *"Seet! Seet!"* Other chaffinches quickly hide in trees and bushes where the hawk can't see them.

Animal noises aren't words. Animals can't talk, as we do. But many sounds that animals make really do say something.

Coyote

When a coyote howls, others usually
begin to howl, too. Some people think
that coyote howls are signals.

When a beaver fears danger it
slaps the water with its tail.
This makes a big splash and a
loud noise. The noise warns
other beavers of danger. When
they hear it, they hurry into
the water and swim away.

Beaver

A long winter nap

In the autumn, a woodchuck curls up into a ball in its underground home and goes to sleep. And it sleeps during the whole winter.

The woodchuck's sleep isn't like the sleep you have at night. The woodchuck's heart slows down and nearly stops. The woodchuck's breathing nearly stops, too. And the woodchuck's body changes. Most of the time the woodchuck's body is warm because it is a warm-blooded animal. But the woodchuck's body grows cold before it goes into its winter sleep.

The woodchuck's sleep is called hibernation. Ground squirrels, bats, and some other warm-blooded animals also hibernate. Bears, and some other animals take long naps in winter, but they don't really hibernate. Their bodies don't get cold.

Snakes, turtles, frogs, and toads hibernate too, but in a different way. A snake is cold-blooded. Its body is always just as warm or cold as the air around it. So as the weather grows colder a snake's body grows colder. The snake tries to get warm by crawling into a hole. The weather gets colder and the snake's body gets colder and stiff. Its heart and breathing nearly stop.

The snake must wait until warm weather comes before its body warms up enough so that it can move. But the woodchuck's body warms up by itself, long before warm weather comes. There's often snow still on the ground when the woodchuck wakes up and scampers out of its hole.

Woodchuck

A woodchuck sleeps all
winter in its underground
home. This kind of long
sleep is called hibernation.

In winter a snake's body gets
so cold and stiff it can't move
until warm weather comes. This
is a kind of hibernation, too.

Water Snake

Migrating Birds

The great mystery

Hundreds of barn swallows sit in rows on telephone wires. Suddenly, with a great twittering, they all rush into the air. Staying close together in a big flock, they fly away. It is late summer and the barn swallows have begun to migrate.

Every autumn millions of geese, ducks, storks, cuckoos, bobolinks, and other birds migrate. They leave the north, where they spent the summer, and fly south. Sometimes many birds fly together. Some birds fly alone.

When birds migrate they often fly thousands of miles. Sometimes they cross oceans and mountains. But the birds always go to the same warm parts of the world where their ancestors have gone for thousands of years. The birds stay all winter in these warm places. In the spring they migrate back to the north. Sometimes they even go back to the same nests they used the summer before.

Birds aren't the only animals that migrate. Monarch butterflies, ladybugs, and many other insects migrate, too. So do some fish and mammals.

It is usually still warm when birds and insects begin to migrate. How do they know winter is coming? How do they know where to go? What makes them always go to the same place?

Scientists know that something in a bird's or insect's body makes it leave at the right time and steers it the way it should go. But no one is sure of all the causes. Migration is a great mystery!

Helpful animals

Crocodiles try to eat most birds that come near them. But one kind of bird can walk about among crocodiles and be quite safe. In fact, these birds even lay their eggs in the same place where the crocodiles lay their eggs!

The birds are called water dikkops and they eat insects that bother the crocodiles. Of course, this gives the birds an easy meal, but it also makes the crocodiles more comfortable. So the birds are really helping the crocodiles and maybe that's why the crocodiles don't harm them.

Other birds, called tickbirds, help the rhinoceros. A rhinoceros usually won't let other kinds of animals near it. But it lets tickbirds ride on its back! Tiny insects on the rhinoceros' back bite it and make it itch, and the tickbird eats these insects. This makes the rhinoceros feel better.

Little fish called wrasses help many other fish. Tiny worms often fasten themselves to a fish and make sores on its body. When this happens the fish goes to a coral reef where a wrasse lives. The little wrasse hunts all over the fish's body and eats all the worms.

The water dikkop, the tickbird, and the wrasse are all getting something from the animals they help. They are getting food. And the animals they help are getting rid of pests that bother them and cause them pain. Scientists call this mutualism.

Tickbirds and Black Rhinoceros

The tickbirds help the
rhinoceros by eating insects
that bother it.

The little cleaner fish are
helping the big fish by eating
tiny worms that are on it.

Cleaner Fish

Safety in numbers

A herd of baboons hunts for food at the edge of a grassy plain in Africa. Each baboon is looking and listening every second. There might be a lion creeping through the grass toward them!

If a baboon sees or hears something, it gives a loud grunt. It sounds almost like a man yelling "Hah!" Then all the baboons hurry to climb trees. Because of one baboon's warning, all the baboons are safe.

Some animals live together in herds. They are safer that way. An animal by itself may not see or hear the enemy that creeps toward it. But if there are many animals together, there are many more chances that one animal will see or smell danger and warn the others.

Baboons

Musk Oxen and Wolves

When the musk oxen are in a
circle, wolves don't dare attack.

Herds of baboons, zebras, antelopes, and deer run
when they are warned of danger. But sometimes a whole
herd of animals will fight an enemy.

When big, shaggy musk oxen in Canada are attacked
by wolves, the musk oxen quickly get into a circle with
the babies on the inside. The musk oxen stand with their
big heads down. Their sharp horns point out at the
wolves. The wolves snarl and growl but they don't dare
attack. As long as the musk oxen stay in their circle the
whole herd is safe.

Sometimes one animal by itself isn't as safe as it is in
a herd. There's safety in numbers!

A wood-ant city

An ant nest is like a little city where hundreds or even thousands of ants live together. Ants make their nests by digging tunnels and storerooms in the ground.

The picture on the page across from this one shows a wood-ant nest. If you look at the picture carefully, you can see a lot going on. On the ground above the nest a group of workers hunts for food. The ant with wings is a male. Male ants don't do any work.

Inside the nest, in the top tunnel, two workers are bringing in part of a leaf. They will use it to repair the nest. Other workers are getting ready to carry cocoons to another room. Inside each cocoon is a baby ant. When the babies grow up they will break out of the cocoons and go right to work.

In the next tunnel is the queen ant. She is much bigger than the workers. She spends her whole life laying eggs. She is the mother of all the ants in the nest.

Ants work together as if they were quite smart. But they aren't really smart. They can't think about things as you can. An ant does things because its body gets signals, such as smells. Different smells make ants do different things.

Ants never change or learn anything new. They can't. Hundreds of millions of years ago ants were living the same way and doing the same sort of things they do now.

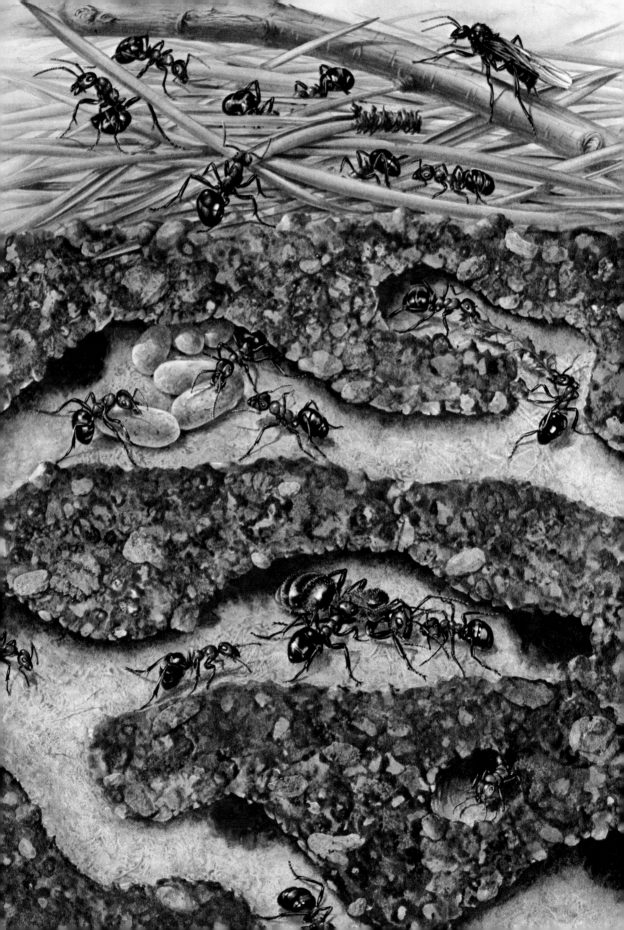

Otter

Otters love to play on slides. This
otter made a slide of the snowbank.
In summertime, otters like to slide
down muddy riverbanks into the water.

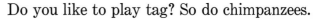

Animal games

Do you like to play tag? So do chimpanzees.

Chimpanzees chase each other in and out among trees and bushes, screaming and chattering. They look as if they're angry but they're really having fun. Sometimes, as if to start a game, a young chimpanzee pinches another and runs away!

Seals love to play, too. They snort and bark and splash and play tag in the water.

Chimpanzees, seals, and many other animals seem to play just for fun, as you do. But when many baby animals play, they are learning things at the same time. They are exercising their bodies and learning how to hunt.

Wolf cubs play by rushing at each other. They snap and growl and try to knock each other down. When they are older, they hunt by running after other animals and trying to knock them down.

Fox pups learn by playing, too. When one is lying down, another will creep slowly toward it and jump on its tail. When they are grown, foxes get food the same way, by creeping toward an animal and jumping upon it.

Many baby mammals play for fun and to learn things. But baby insects, reptiles, amphibians, and fish never seem to play. They are too busy trying to find food and trying to keep from being eaten.

The Animals' World

To a fennec fox, the world is filled with sounds.

We see, hear, smell, and feel the world around us. So do animals. But many animals do these things in different ways. Some kinds of animals can't do all of them. Some kinds of animals do them better than others.

So, for each kind of animal, the world is different. Some animals see colors, other animals see only shades of gray. For some animals the world is filled with smells, for others there are no smells at all. Some animals can't hear. Some can't see at all.

For some kinds of animals the world is *very* different. A bat's world is darkness filled with echoing sound. For a butterfly the world is filled with shapes and colors and smells we can hardly imagine.

But each kind of animal has exactly the right kind of eyes, or nose, or ears, or feelers, or tail, or other things it needs to find its way and live its life in its world.

A painted lady butterfly smells its world through its feelers.

The great horned owl's big eyes can see clearly in the dark. ▶

The long-tailed woolly monkey can live in a world of treetops.

What animals see

If you were a rabbit, nibbling plants in a meadow, you would be able to see in front, on both sides, and nearly all the way behind—all at the same time!

But you wouldn't see any color at all. Everything would be gray and fuzzy, like a black-and-white TV picture that isn't tuned in just right. But if something moved behind you, you would see the movement at once.

If you were a hawk, you would see things in colors, just as people do. But your eyes would be like magnifying glasses. A hawk

A hawk's eyesight is about eight times stronger than a person's eyesight. It can see a mouse running in grass 1,000 feet away.

Broadwinged Hawk

Deer

Because a deer's eyes are on the sides of its head, a deer can see in front, on both sides, and partway behind itself all at the same time.

Dragonfly's eyes

Most insects' eyes are made up of thousands of tiny eyes. Each tiny eye sees a piece of what the insect looks at.

These are pictures of the same flower. The bottom picture was taken with a special kind of light. It shows that there's a color we can't see in the middle of the flower. A bee sees this color as a bright glow.

flying 1,000 feet in the air can see a tiny mouse running in the grass below.

If you could see through a bee's eyes things would look most strange to you. A field of red flowers would seem like a big, black shadow. Yellow daisies would have glowing spots that people can't see. The glowing spots are a color called ultraviolet. Bees see ultraviolet, but people cannot.

Many other animals see things very differently from the way people do. Some spiders have eight eyes! What do you suppose things look like to them? How do things look to a lobster or an octopus? We can only guess. But each kind of animal sees the way it must, to stay alive.

Listen!

A bat flies through a cave. Long, sharp rocks hang from the roof. Other rocks stick up from the floor. The cave is darker than night and you wouldn't see a thing. But the bat doesn't bump into a single rock.

How does the bat tell where the rocks are? It hears them!

As the bat flies, it makes tiny squeaks. If a rock is ahead of the bat, the squeak makes an echo. The bat hears the echo and knows something is there. He flies around it. You couldn't hear either the bat's squeaks or the echo. A bat's ears can hear sounds that yours can't.

Birds can hear better than humans, too. Have you ever seen a thrush or blackbird stand with its head to one side? It's listening to a worm crawl! The bird hops toward the noise and pulls the worm from its hole. A bird's ears are two little holes, one on each side of its head.

A bat makes tiny squeaks as it flies
in the dark. If it hears the squeaks
bounce back, the bat knows something
is in its way and flies around it.

Horseshoe Bat

Deer, big-eared rabbits, and many other animals need good hearing to keep from being eaten. They can move their ears to listen for the tiny noises that may mean a wolf, bobcat, or other enemy is near.

Dogs can also hear sounds that you can't hear. If you blow on a special dog whistle, you won't hear a thing. But your dog will. And he'll come running.

Boston Bull Terrier

Say a dog's name very softly and you'll see his ears move. Dogs and some other mammals can point their ears toward the sounds they hear.

Flying Squirrel

The squirrel can tell if the hickory nut is good or bad by the way it smells.

A world of smells

Even though you can't see them, you can tell when cookies are baking nearby. You can't see perfume on a lady, but you can tell she's wearing it. And you know if someone has been eating peppermint if they stand close to you. Your nose tells you all these things.

An animal's nose tells it many things, too. In fact, most animals' noses tell them a lot more than your nose tells you. A squirrel sniffs at a nut before carrying the nut home. If you sniffed at the nut you might not smell anything at all. But the squirrel's nose tells the squirrel if the nut is good or rotten.

When a snake pokes its tongue out it is smelling. A snake's tongue helps it smell things.

Israeli Racer

When a snake goes hunting it pokes its Y-shaped tongue in and out. A snake's tongue can find the smell of a mouse or frog even in a whole forest of other smells. The snake follows the smell by sticking its tongue in and out.

Insects can smell things very well even though they have no noses. An insect smells with its two wiggly feelers. A male luna moth has feelers like two golden feathers. These feelers can smell a female luna moth that is as much as a mile away!

Smell helps an animal find food or find a mate. Smell lets an animal know that an enemy is near. Each animal lives in its own world of smells—and every smell means something to it.

With its two feathery, golden feelers, this moth can smell another moth that is nearly a mile away.

Luna Moth

A different way of hunting

A hungry rattlesnake glides through the grass at night. The animals it hunts can't see it well in the dark. The snake can't see them either, but it doesn't have to. It has another way of finding them.

On the rattlesnake's head, just below its eyes, are two openings called pits. These pits can feel the warmth of another animal's body—even though the animal is not very near.

Suddenly, the snake turns to the left. A rat is nearby and the rattlesnake's pits have felt the heat of the rat's warm body. Silently the snake moves closer. Then it shoots its head forward and catches the rat in its mouth. The snake's pits guided the snake right to where the rat was!

Below each eye on a rattlesnake's head is a hole called a pit. The rattlesnake's pits help it find the animals it eats.

Banded Rattlesnake and Wood Rat

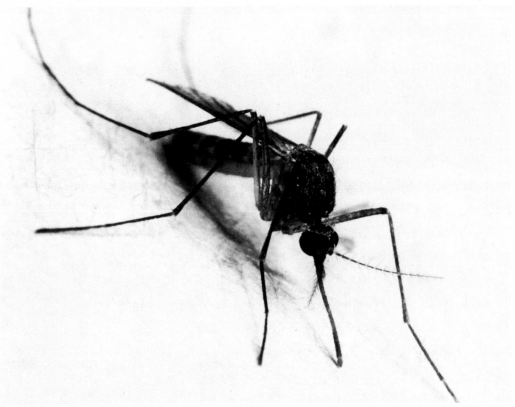

Female Mosquito

On a female mosquito's round,
knoblike head are two feelers
that help her find her food.

A female mosquito can feel warmth a long way off, too.
She feels heat with her two wiggly feelers. The blood of
warm animals is a female mosquito's food. When a mosquito comes onto your arm, her feelers have told her you
were warm—and she wants to eat!

We know what it's like for an animal to hunt by seeing,
hearing, and smelling. But what would it be like to hunt
by feeling an animal's warmth a long way off, as rattlesnakes and mosquitoes do? That's part of the world of
animals that we can only imagine.

The night world

A mouse scampers through the grass in a meadow. It is night and only the stars are out. The mouse can hardly see. But the mouse knows its way, for this part of the meadow is its territory. It finds its way in the dark as easily as you walk through the rooms of your house. The air is full of smells and the mouse sniffs at them as it runs. It uses its nose to find food.

Not far away a big-eyed owl sits in a tree. Big eyes let in more light. That's why an owl can see better in the dark than a day animal could. The owl can't see the mouse, though. The night is too dark. But suddenly the owl flies straight toward the mouse. The owl can hear so well that it hears even the tiny sound of the mouse running! The mouse squeaks as the owl's claws snatch it up!

In another part of the meadow, a racoon sniffs the air and listens for sounds. The raccoon's eyes glow like yellow fire. There are things like little mirrors inside the raccoon's eyes. The glow is made by moonlight and star-light shining on the "mirrors." Many night animals have mirrorlike eyes to help them see better in the dark.

A meadow or a forest at night is often busier than it is in daytime. It's filled with moths, fireflies, bats, owls, whippoorwills, foxes, raccoons, and other animals. All night long these night animals hunt and eat in their world of darkness, sounds, and smells.

Great Horned Owl and Mouse

The owl has caught a mouse and will eat
it. Owls and mice are night animals.

Hot and cold

A kangaroo rat's world is the burning hot desert.

The desert is baked by the sun. The air above the sand is so hot it wiggles! During the day, a kangaroo rat sleeps in a cool, underground hole. There it is safe from the terrible heat.

When the sun goes down, the desert cools. Then the rat comes out. It scampers about, looking for seeds that blow across the desert. The rat doesn't look for water. Even if there were water, the kangaroo rat wouldn't drink it. The kangaroo rat never drinks! Its body is able to make the water it needs out of just the dry seeds the rat eats.

Kangaroo rats live in deserts. These rats never drink water. They stay in their cool, underground homes during the hot day.

Kangaroo Rat

Walruses

Walruses live where it's always
cold and icy. But a walrus is
kept warm by the thick fat
under its skin.

A walrus lives in a world of cold water and floating islands of ice.

A walrus swims to the edge of an ice island and sticks
his two, long front teeth, called tusks, into the ice. He
pulls himself right out of the water with his tusks. Then
he lies on the ice in the sunshine, just as you would lie
on a sandy beach. Thick, tough skin with lots of thick
fat underneath helps keep the walrus warm.

Differences in each animal's body help it stay alive in
its world. A kangaroo rat has what it needs to stay alive
in a hot desert. A walrus has what it needs to stay alive
in its cold, icy world. A kangaroo rat and a walrus could
never change places with each other.

Trunks and tails

Wouldn't it seem strange to have a hand on the end of your nose? But an elephant has a sort of hand on the end of its nose.

The elephant's trunk is its nose. And at the end of the trunk are one or two little bumps that the elephant can use as fingers. An elephant can reach up with its trunk and tear leaves from a tree. Then the elephant curls its trunk down and stuffs the leaves into its mouth. An elephant can pick up a tiny peanut with its trunk. And an elephant can use its trunk like a club, to hit a tiger and knock it head over heels!

Woolly monkeys, howler monkeys, and some other kinds of South American monkeys have tails that are nearly as handy as an elephant's trunk. These monkeys use their tails to catch hold of branches as the monkeys swing through the trees. One of these monkeys can hang by its tail from a branch and pull fruit from another branch with its hands. Having that kind of tail is just like having an extra arm!

African Elephant

An elephant uses the tip
of its trunk like a hand.

Howler Monkey

This monkey can
use its tail as an extra arm.

Curiosities

Platypus

The platypus, or duckbill, is a mammal,
but it seems to be part bird, too. It has
a body like a beaver and a bill and feet
like a duck. A mother platypus gives
milk, as all mammal mothers do. But she
also lays eggs, as all bird mothers do!

Echidna

The echidna is a mammal, but it's mixed-
up just like the platypus. A mother
echidna gives milk, as mammal mothers do.
But she also lays eggs, like a bird.
The echidna is also called a spiny
anteater. It eats ants and termites.

Curiosities

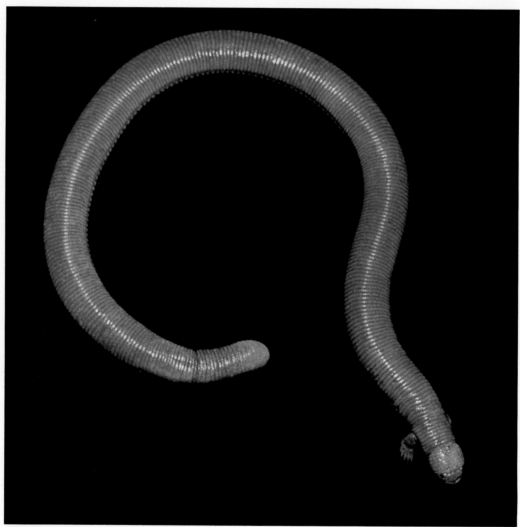

Ajolote

The strange lizard called an ajolote
looks like a worm with two legs! It
uses its two tiny legs to help it
crawl and to dig underground holes
where it hides during the day.
Ajolotes are found only in Lower
California.

Glass Snake

The glass snake isn't made of glass.
It isn't even a snake. It's a lizard—
without legs. You can tell it isn't a
snake because it has eyelids. No real
snake has eyelids. If you picked up a
glass snake by the tail, its tail would
break off! Many lizards have tails that
break off and grow again. But snakes don't.

Curiosities

Walking Fish

This fish will drown if it stays
underwater too long! It has to come to
the top of the water once in a while
to gulp air. Sometimes it even crawls
out of the water! It walks on land,
pulling itself along with its fins.

Sometimes the lakes and streams where
lungfish live, dry up. This would kill
other fish. But a lungfish just builds
a shell of mud around itself and goes
to sleep—until the lake fills up
again and the mud softens. Lungfish
can breathe in both water and air.

African Lungfish

The biggest and the smallest

This ruler will help you see how big or how small each of these animals is.

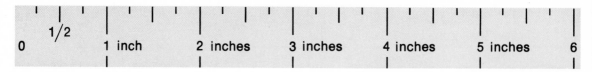

| 0 | 1/2 | 1 inch | 2 inches | 3 inches | 4 inches | 5 inches | 6 |

Mammals

The Etruscan shrew is as long as 1 inch on the ruler. The blue whale is as long as 100 rulers in a row. The shrew and the whale are both mammals. And so is a collie dog.

The Etruscan shrew is the smallest mammal. It's no longer than a man's thumb.

The blue whale is the biggest mammal. It's as long as eight elephants in a row.

Birds

The bee hummingbird is as long as 2 inches on the ruler. The ostrich is as tall as eight rulers in a row. The hummingbird and the ostrich are both birds. And so is a sparrow.

The ostrich is the biggest bird. It's taller than a tall man.

The bee hummingbird is the smallest bird. It's no longer than one of your fingers.

Reptiles

The West Indian gecko is as long as 2 inches on the ruler. The reticulated python is as long as 30 rulers in a row. The gecko and the python are both reptiles. So is a turtle.

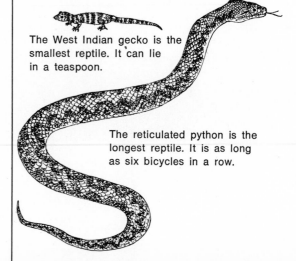

The West Indian gecko is the smallest reptile. It can lie in a teaspoon.

The reticulated python is the longest reptile. It is as long as six bicycles in a row.

```
inches    7 inches    8 inches    9 inches    10 inches    11 inches    12
```

Amphibians

The Cuban arrow-poison frog is as long as ½ inch on the ruler. The giant salamander is as long as five rulers in a row. The salamander and frog are both amphibians. So is a toad.

The Cuban arrow-poison frog is the smallest amphibian. It's about the size of a dime.

The giant salamander is the biggest amphibian. It's about as long as a bicycle.

Fish

The dwarf pygmy goby is as long as ½ inch on the ruler. The whale shark is as long as 50 rulers in a row. The goby and the whale shark are both fish. So is a goldfish.

The dwarf pygmy goby is the smallest fish. It's no longer than a man's fingernail.

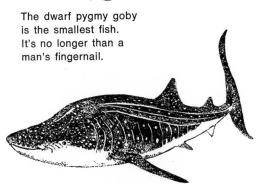

The whale shark is the biggest fish. It's a little longer than a railroad train boxcar.

Arthropods

A mite is smaller than this dot. A giant spider crab is as wide as eight rulers in a row. The mite and the spider crab are both arthropods. And so is an ant.

A mite is the smallest arthropod. The smallest mites are so tiny you can't see them without a microscope.

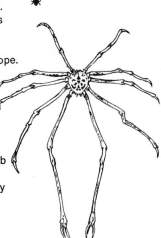

A giant spider crab is the biggest arthropod. Its body is as big as a basketball.

Living Together

A monarch butterfly caterpillar can live wherever there are milkweed plants.

· Everywhere in the world, different kinds of plants and animals live together.

Some animals eat plants they live with. Some animals eat other animals they live with. Some animals move far in search of food. Some animals stay near the same place. But all these animals and plants are important to each other—and to us!

If it weren't for some insects, many kinds of plants could not have seeds. If many plant-eating animals didn't have natural enemies that eat them, the plants would be destroyed. If there were no worms and other tiny creatures that live underground there would be no rich soil for the roots of plants. And if there were no green plants, there would be no animals —and no people.

It takes all the plants and animals living together to keep the earth a good place for them—and us—to live in.

A grasshopper mouse helps keep the number of grasshoppers down.

A giant panda lives only where bamboo plants grow. ▶

A wolverine is the natural enemy of many animals.

Plants and animals need each other

Plants and animals trade with each other. They trade for things they both need to stay alive.

Animals breathe air. The air gets changed inside their bodies. When they breathe the air out again there's something called carbon in it. Animals can't use this air again. But plants need carbon. They take the carbon out of the air—and then animals can breathe the air again. The plants trade fresh air for the carbon they need.

Plants make food from carbon and water. They use sunlight for this work, just as a machine uses gasoline or electricity to keep running. The plants store the food they make inside themselves. Many animals eat plants and then the animals' bodies store up the food that was in the plants. Other animals, such as foxes, wolves, and lions, eat animals that eat plants and get the plant food that's stored in the animals' bodies. So plants are really feeding all animals.

But what do the plants get in return? Many things. Plants make food from the carbon and other things that come from animals' bodies. The animals we call insects carry pollen from one flower to another and the pollen forms seeds. Birds and other animals eat the fruit in which seeds grow and often drop the seeds where they can sprout into new plants. So animals help make new plants grow.

Plants and animals need each other. They couldn't stay alive without each other.

Bumblebee

As a bee gets food from a flower, yellow
dust called pollen falls on its body.
The pollen rubs off on other flowers the
bee goes to, and makes new seeds grow.

Why animals live where they do

You eat bacon and cereal for breakfast. A bear eats fish and berries. Some kinds of animals eat only food from plants. Some kinds eat only other animals. Some animals eat both kinds of food. But each kind of animal has its favorite food and must live where it can get what it needs.

Cows eat grass. Zebras and gazelles do, too. So they do not live in the forest, but on big plains where there is plenty of grass to eat. Lions eat gazelles and zebras. So lions live on the big plains, too, where they will be near their kind of food.

Giant pandas live in the mountains in Southern China. The pandas eat young bamboo plants. The kind of

Plant eaters, such as zebras, live where the plants they eat grow. Meat eaters, such as cheetahs, live where the plant eaters do.

Cheetahs and Zebras

bamboo the pandas eat grows only in the mountains where the pandas live. The pandas couldn't move to another part of China. There would be no food for them in another place.

Koalas live in Australia. They eat only the leaves of 12 kinds of eucalyptus trees. And the koalas can eat only a few of the leaves on each tree. So a koala must live where there are plenty of eucalyptus trees.

Meat-eating animals must live near the animals they eat. Plant-eating animals must live near the plants they eat. And each kind of plant must live in the place that's just right for it. That's why, everywhere in the world, some kinds of plants and animals always live together.

Nature's clean-up crew

What becomes of the leaves that fall in the forest every autumn? What keeps them from piling up each year and covering the world with leaves?

Each spring, millions of baby insects eat into the leaves that lie on the ground. Mold grows inside the leaves, making them rot. The leaves begin to fall apart.

Earthworms, insects called springtails, and tiny spiderlike mites go to work. They chew and grind the leaves into pieces. The leaves are digested and pass out of their bodies and into the ground as waste. Mold and very tiny creatures called bacteria change the waste into gas and liquid. And by next fall, nothing is left of most of last year's leaves.

The insects, earthworms, mold, and bacteria are nature's clean-up crew. They're mighty important to us, for without them the world would be a big garbage dump! They help get rid of every dead thing from autumn leaves to elephants.

But the clean-up crew does even more than just get rid of garbage. The clean-up crew turns all dead plants and animals into things that plants can use. The gas and liquid that dead, rotting things become is needed by plants. Without it they couldn't grow or live. And without plants there could be no animals or people.

Without the crawling animals and the mold and bacteria of the clean-up crew—we couldn't live!

Slugs and baby insects live in fallen leaves. Below the leaves live mites and springtails, shown in circles. Worms and mole crickets live farther down.

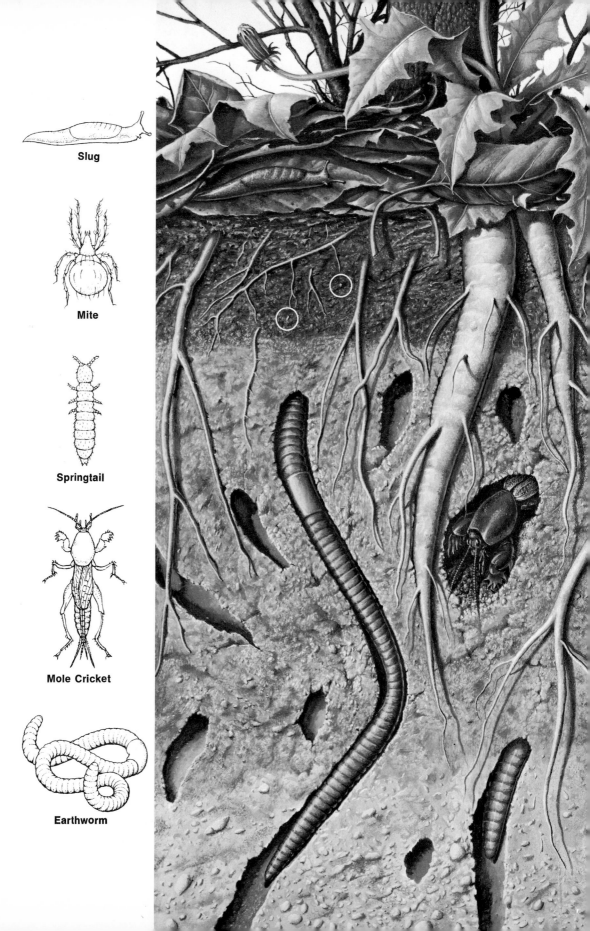

Slug

Mite

Springtail

Mole Cricket

Earthworm

Life in low places and high places

Underground caves are blacker than a lump of coal. Mountaintops are cold and bare. It doesn't seem possible for animals to live in these places. But animals do live in them.

Small, white fish swim in a stream in an underground cave. The fish have no eyes! There is no light at all in the cave, so eyes would be of no use to the fish.

But even though they are blind, the fish never bump into anything or each other. These fish can feel things in the water before they touch them.

One of the fish swims toward the side of the cave. A tiny, eyeless, pale crayfish is hanging from a rock. The fish rushes forward and gulps down the crayfish. The fish can feel and smell so well that it can find food easily.

On a mountaintop far, far above the cave, a Rocky Mountain goat is looking for plants to eat. The goat climbs higher and higher. The way is steep and narrow, but the goat climbs easily. Its cuplike hoofs keep it from slipping. The goat can go where no other animal can follow. The goat is right at home on the high, steep mountaintop.

Millions of years ago animals moved into every place in the world where they could go. That's why today there are animals living in even the highest and lowest places. And the animals all changed to fit the places where they lived. That's why Rocky Mountain goats don't slip and cave fish don't need eyes.

Rocky Mountain Goat

A mountain goat can climb to the highest, narrowest parts of a mountain. Its hoofs keep it from slipping.

The cave fish has no eyes. It doesn't need them in its coal-black world. It finds its food by feel and smell.

Cave Fish

Keep out!

Some animals hunt for food in many different places and sleep wherever they happen to be. But other animals always sleep and hunt in the same place. This place is their territory.

A dragonfly's territory is a space about as big as a room. An owl's territory may be a meadow or part of a woods. An ape family's territory is usually several hundred trees in a jungle. Even some kinds of fish have territories in which they swim about and never leave.

Most animals guard their territories. Some of them even put "Keep Out" signs on the edges of their territories. Deer, bears, and many other animals rub against trees and leave a smell that says "Keep Out" to others. A wolverine puts a "Keep Off" smell on any food it finds, but doesn't eat, in its territory. The songs of many birds are a way of saying "Keep out of my territory" to other birds.

If too many of the same kind of animals lived in one territory, there might not be enough food for all. So most animals try to keep animals like themselves out of their territory. Some animals won't even let their own young stay in the territory after they grow up.

Animals don't seem to mind if different kinds of animals share their territory. But if an animal like themselves tries to move in—they will fight to keep it out.

Mockingbirds defend their
territory. So when this owl
came into its territory, the
mockingbird attacked.

With a hard peck the mockingbird lets the surprised owl
know that it better keep out
of mockingbird territory.

Mockingbird and Great Horned Owl

Keeping things even

Once, several thousand deer and a few dozen mountain lions lived together in a part of Arizona. Each year, the mountain lions ate hundreds of deer. But, during the year, hundreds of new deer were born. So there was always just about the same number of deer. And there was always just about the same number of mountain lions.

There weren't too many mountain lions, so they always had plenty to eat. There weren't too many deer, so the deer had plenty to eat. Everything was even.

Then, the mountain lions killed some farm animals. The farmers began to hunt the mountain lions. Soon, the mountain lions there had all been killed.

After that, baby deer that would have been killed by mountain lions were able to grow up. Many of them had babies. Soon, there were many more deer than there had been when the mountain lions were eating them. Things weren't even any more.

Now there were so many deer that there wasn't enough food for all of them.

In the summer, they ate up most of the food that would have kept them alive during the winter.

And when winter came, thousands of the deer starved to death.

Animals keep things even by living together. As long as things are even, the animals are all right. But sometimes men change things so they're no longer even, and then there is trouble for the animals—and often for people, too.

Mule Deer

Natural enemies

Most animals have natural enemies—other animals that like to eat them.

It's night on a desert in the United States. A wolf spider is hunting. The spider is the natural enemy of beetles and other insects.

The spider, hurrying over the sand, meets a scorpion. And the scorpion is the spider's natural enemy. With its two front claws the scorpion grabs the spider. The scorpion's long tail flashes down and its sharp sting stabs into the spider. Then the scorpion begins to eat the spider.

After a while the scorpion finishes. A bright-eyed grass-hopper mouse comes around a rock. The mouse sees the scorpion. The mouse dashes forward and bites off the scorpion's poisonous tail. Then the mouse pushes the scorpion into its mouth. This kind of mouse is the natural enemy of the scorpion.

The mouse cleans its whiskers and trots off. Suddenly, something swoops through the air. It's a screech owl—the mouse's natural enemy. The owl grabs the mouse with its sharp claws.

Few other animals hunt owls to eat, so the owl is safe from natural enemies. So are wolves, bears, lions, tigers, and other big meat-eating animals. Old age is their worst enemy. For when a hunting animal gets too old to move quickly, it can't catch anything. Then it starves to death.

Scorpion and Spider

The yellow scorpion has caught the
brown spider and will eat it. A
scorpion is a spider's natural enemy.

Change or die!

Suppose that all the milkweed plants in the world suddenly died. What would happen to monarch butterfly caterpillars? They eat only milkweed leaves.

The mother monarch butterflies would have to lay their eggs on another kind of plant. And the caterpillars would have to learn to eat the leaves of that plant. Otherwise the caterpillars would die, and soon there would be no monarch butterflies.

If the monarch butterflies changed, and learned to eat another kind of plant, we would say they had adapted. And if they didn't change, and all died, we would say they were extinct.

Millions of years ago giant reptiles called dinosaurs were everywhere. Maybe the world got too cold for them. Maybe something happened to their food. But whatever happened, the dinosaurs weren't able to adapt. There are no dinosaurs alive today. They are all extinct.

Millions of years ago there were tiny horses with toes instead of hoofs. They lived in forests and ate leaves. Then something happened. Maybe there wasn't enough food. Maybe the forests became too dangerous. But the horses learned to live on the plains and eat grass. They adapted.

The horses of today came from those long-ago horses that adapted. In fact, every kind of animal in the world today came from animals that adapted, long, long ago.

Eohippus

The top picture shows what horses were
like millions of years ago. They were
no bigger than cats! But they were
the ancestors of today's big horses
like the one in the picture below.

Arabian Stallion

Animals of Long Ago

Imagine animals like fish with legs. Imagine trees like giant feather dusters. That's what some animals and trees looked like, once.

The world is very old. Just as you change as you grow older, the world changes and the things that live on it change. The world has changed many times in the past. And many kinds of animals have lived on it.

Once there were scaly reptiles as big as houses. Once there were horses no bigger than cats. And once, very long ago, there were no animals of any kind living on the land. All the animals lived in water.

The next few pages will show you some of the strange animals that lived on the earth long ago.

The pteranodon was a flying reptile.

Tyrannosaurus was a big reptile.

The mammoth was a mammal.

Triceratops was a reptile. ▶

Strange sea animals

Five hundred million years ago all plants and animals lived in the sea. There were sponges, jellyfish, worms with legs, and things like clams.

And there was another animal that moved busily everywhere over the rocks and sand. It had big, buglike eyes and feelers and many legs. It looked like a crab and insect mixed together. This animal was a trilobite.

Some trilobites were as big as your fist. Most were no bigger than a quarter. They were no smarter than insects. But 500 million years ago, trilobites were the biggest and smartest animals in the whole world.

Use this small picture
to find out the names of the
animals in the big picture.

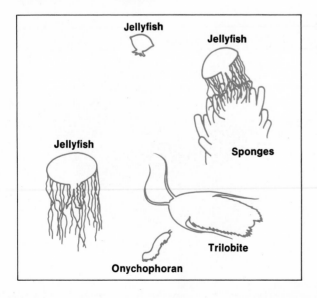

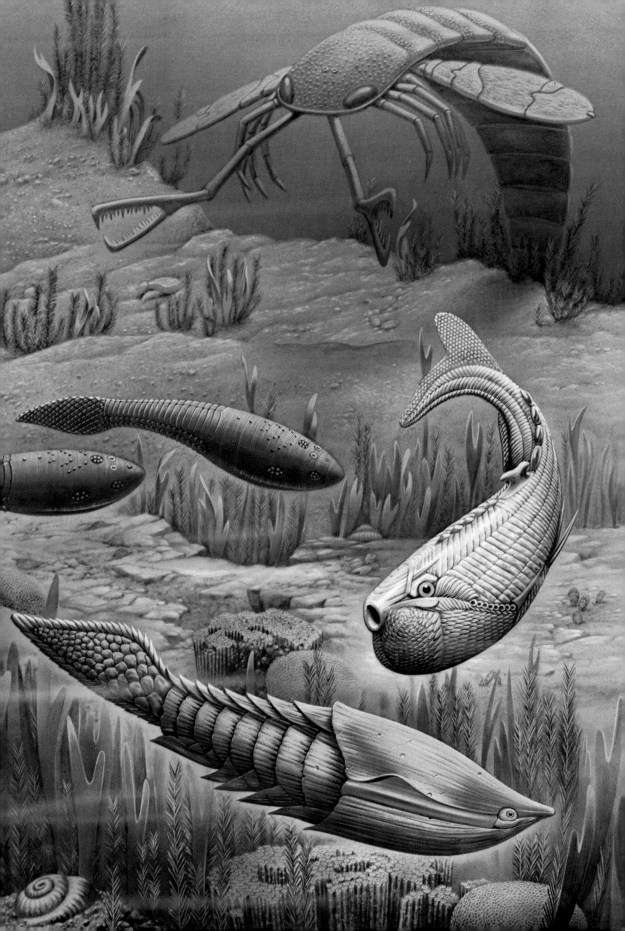

Fish in armor

The fishes that swam in the seas 430 million years ago were covered with hard, bony armor. They had no jaws like the fish of today. Their mouths were just holes in the bony shells that covered their heads. They sucked food through the holes as they swam slowly over the sea-bottom.

The armored fish weren't the only animals in the water. There were creatures with many legs, like insects. They were big and fast and they ate other animals. The armored fish were smaller and slower. They needed their armor for protection.

Use this small picture
to find out the names of the
animals in the big picture.

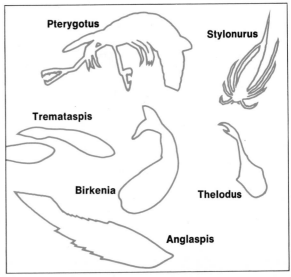

Pterygotus

Stylonurus

Tremataspis

Birkenia

Thelodus

Anglaspis

Fish that crawled

Imagine a fish—with legs!

There really were such animals! About 400 million years ago, fish with legs swam in the warm, green seas and crawled around on the muddy land. They were the first four-footed animals in the world.

Use this small picture
to find out the names of the
animals in the big picture.

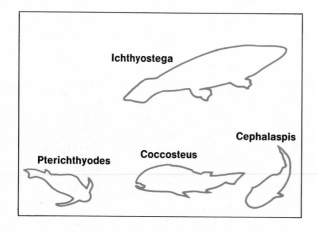

Ichthyostega

Cephalaspis

Pterichthyodes   Coccosteus

A 250 million year old puzzle

About 250 million years ago there lived a big reptile called dimetrodon. It was about as long as a small automobile. It ate smaller reptiles.

Dimetrodon is a puzzle to scientists. It had a big fin like a sail on its back. No one knows what this was for.

Some fishes of today have big fins on their backs. The fins help them swim. But dimetrodon wasn't a water animal. It couldn't have used the fin for swimming.

Some scientists think the fin helped keep dimetrodon from getting too hot or too cold. But no one is really sure what the fin was for.

Dimetrodon

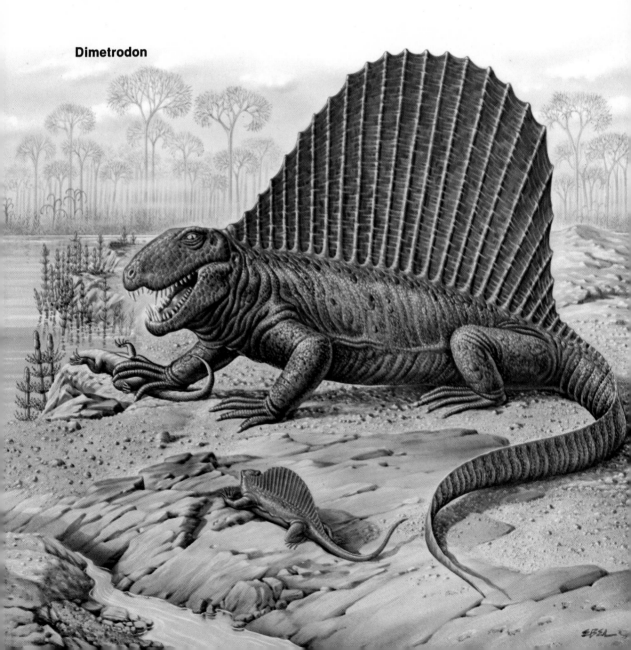

Coelophysis

Turtles and terrible lizards

About 225 million years ago, the first dinosaurs came into the world. And along with them came the first turtles.

The word *dinosaur* means *terrible lizard*. But the first dinosaurs weren't very terrible. Some were no bigger than chickens. The biggest were not much taller than a tall man. It wasn't until millions of years later that there were giant dinosaurs.

The first turtles looked much like turtles do now. Turtles' shapes must be just right for them. They haven't changed much in 225 million years.

Triassochelys

The biggest dinosaurs

You could have walked beneath a brontosaurus—and your head wouldn't even have touched its stomach.

A brontosaurus was as long as four big elephants standing in a line. The word *brontosaurus* means *thunder lizard*. The man who named it thought that when such a big animal walked, it must have made a noise like thunder.

The dinosaur called brachiosaurus was even bigger. It was as long as five big elephants standing in a line. And it was so tall that it could have looked over the top of a four-story building.

These two dinosaurs lived about 150 million years ago. They were big but not dangerous to other animals. They spent most of their lives wading in lakes, stretching their long necks down to fill their mouths with juicy water plants.

Brachiosaurus

Brontosaurus

Flying reptiles

No reptile that lives today—snake, turtle, lizard, alligator, or crocodile—can fly. And no reptile of today has hair on its body. But 150 million years ago there were many flying reptiles. And some scientists think that some of the reptiles may have had a kind of hair on their bodies.

Most of the flying reptiles of 150 million years ago were about the size of bats of today. And the reptiles probably flew much as bats do.

The flying reptiles flapped and fluttered and glided over lakes and seashores and grabbed up fish in their long jaws. They probably climbed trees and hung head down from branches, with their wings folded around themselves like blankets.

Rhamphorhynchus

The first birds

The birds of today sing or whistle or screech. But the first birds may have hissed like snakes! They were more like reptiles than like birds. They were reptiles with wings and feathers.

The first birds we know about were as big as pigeons. They had little claws on their wings and teeth in their mouths. They probably couldn't fly very well, but they could climb trees easily.

The first birds lived about 150 million years ago, at the same time as some of the big dinosaurs.

Archaeopteryx

A fight to the death!

When a tyrannosaurus tried to eat a triceratops there was a terrible, bloody fight.

The tyrannosaurus bit with its six-inch-long teeth and ripped with its sharp claws. The triceratops pushed and jabbed with the three sharp horns on its head. The ground shook as their big, heavy bodies whirled about.

The fight ended only when one of the two dinosaurs was dead.

Triceratops

Tyrannosaurus

Stories in stone

There were no people on the world when dinosaurs were alive. So how do we know about dinosaurs and other animals of long ago?

Sometimes, when a dinosaur died or was killed, its body fell into mud and was covered up. The soft parts of the body rotted away. Only the bones were left.

Slowly, the mud around the bones hardened into rock. The bones rotted away, leaving holes inside the rock. These holes were exactly the same shape as the bones had been.

Mud and sand trickled into the holes through cracks in the rock. The holes filled up. And after a long, long time, the mud and sand inside the holes became rock, too—rock that was exactly the same shape the dinosaur's bones had been.

Scientists look for rocky skeletons such as this and dig them out of the ground. From such a skeleton the scientists can tell what the animal looked like. They can tell what it ate by the shape of its teeth. They can often even tell how well the animal could see and hear and smell things.

Rocky skeletons and bones are called fossils. There are other kinds of fossils, too. Dinosaurs made footprints in mud and the mud turned to stone with the footprints still in it. Insects were caught in gobs of tree sap that turned into a glasslike stone called amber. Fossils such as these are stories in stone that tell us what the animals of long ago were like.

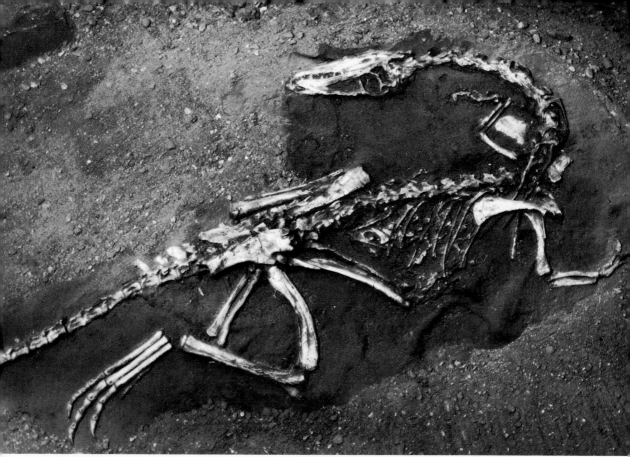

Fossil Skeleton of Dinosaur Coelophysis

Fossil Trilobites and Brachiopods

These are fossils of animals that died and were covered by mud hundreds of millions of years ago. We can tell what the animals looked like from these fossils.

Horses without hoofs

If you could see the horses that lived 65 million years ago, you wouldn't know they were horses. They had toes on their feet instead of hoofs. They ate fruit and leaves instead of grass. And they were no bigger than cats.

Eohippus

Elephants without trunks

Fifty million years ago there were elephants living in swamps where Egypt is today. But they didn't look anything like elephants do now. The first elephants didn't have trunks. They didn't have long tusks. And they were about the size of pigs.

Moeritherium

Mammoth

Elephants with fur coats

If you could have been in North America or Europe twenty thousand years ago, you'd have thought you were at the North Pole! Much of the land was covered with a mountain of ice and snow.

Many animals that lived then were just like the animals that live in cold places today. There were bears, elk, and packs of wolves. There were also animals that looked like huge elephants, but they were covered with thick, shaggy fur. These animals are called *mammoths*, a word that means *very big*.

Mammoths and dinosaurs and many other animals of long ago are all gone. As many years passed, some of those animals died off and others changed. And animals are still changing. In a million years the world will be as different as it was a million years ago. Many of today's animals will be gone. There may be many new kinds of animals. The story of life on earth is a story that is always changing.

Wolf

People and Animals

Some people have jobs working with wild animals! These people work in zoos, parks, animal hospitals, museums, and laboratories. Some even work right in the places where wild animals live.

Zookeepers care for animals in zoos. Some kinds of scientists study animals to learn how they live and act. Veterinarians are animal doctors. Game wardens and rangers care for animals in parks and preserves. And there are artists and photographers who make pictures of animals for books and museums.

There are many kinds of jobs for people who like to work with animals.

**People study animals
to learn more about them.**

**People take care of animals
in zoos and parks.** ▶

**People make pictures of animals
for magazines and books.**

Taking care of zoo animals

Many people work in a zoo. People called keepers feed the animals and keep them and their cages clean. Animal doctors, called veterinarians, check the animals to keep them healthy and care for them if they get sick. Zoologists study the animals to learn more about them. The next few pages show some of the things done by people who work at the famous London Zoo, in England.

An animal can have a toothache, too. Zookeepers check the animals' teeth to make sure they're all right.

Alligator

Elephants must have a bath every day or their skin dries. The elephants play with their keepers and sometimes pull them into the water!

African Elephant

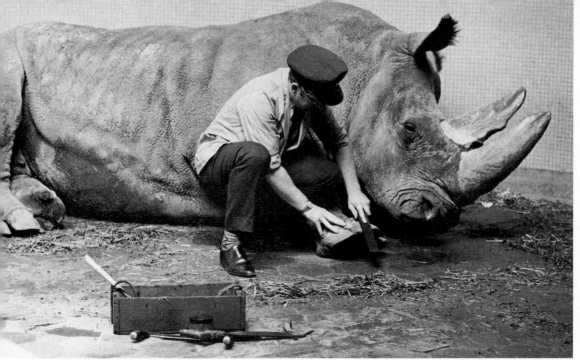

Rhinoceros

A zookeeper cuts and files a
rhinoceros' toenails. If its
toenails grow too long,
the rhinoceros has
trouble walking.

Many animals like to be combed
and brushed by their keepers.
This keeps their coats clean.
Some wild animals keep clean
by rubbing against trees.

Shetland Pony

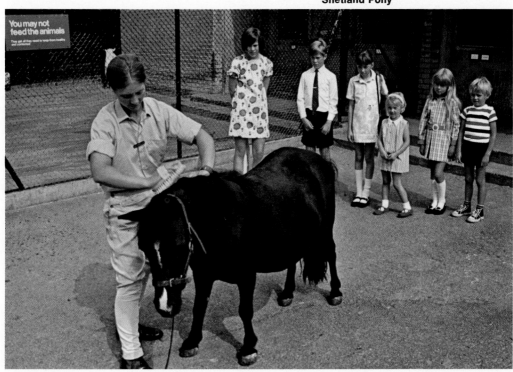

Feeding time

Wild animals can get their own food, but animals in zoos must be fed by keepers. So the keepers have to know what kind of food each animal eats and how much it needs. Feeding the animals is one of the most important parts of taking care of them.

These are dinners for birds. Each tray has chopped fruit, grain, and other things birds like.

A tray of food goes into every bird cage. Each bird gets exactly the right amount of food to keep it healthy.

The zoo must have lots of juicy bamboo plants for the panda every day. That's all a panda eats.

Giant Panda

Lions, tigers, and jaguars don't eat every day in the wild. So they're not fed every day in the zoo, either.

Jaguar

Wild deer never get to eat carrots. But the zookeepers know that carrots are good for a deer.

Red Deer

How do you feed giraffes?

Zoo keepers have to know a lot about each kind of animal so that they can take good care of it. They know that wild giraffes that live in Africa stretch their long necks into trees and eat leaves. This is usually the only way giraffes eat. They can't put their heads down and eat from the ground as many animals do. So zoo keepers have a special way of feeding giraffes.

Here comes a keeper to feed the giraffes. And the giraffes seem to know that it's dinner time.

The keeper fastens a bunch of leaves to a rope that hangs from a tree outside the giraffe house.

The keeper pulls the leaves up into the tree the same way a flag is pulled to the top of a flagpole.

The leaves are just high enough for the giraffes to eat comfortably. And that's how you feed giraffes!

A children's zoo

A children's zoo is a little zoo inside a big one. The animals in a children's zoo are tame and gentle and can be touched and petted. Many of them are babies, so the keepers in a children's zoo must know how to care for baby animals. The keepers must know a lot about all animals, too, because children who visit the zoo ask lots of questions.

There's a tea party for chimpanzees every afternoon at the London Zoo.

Chimpanzees

Goat

Zookeepers must know a lot about
animals. This girl zookeeper is
telling children about a goat.

Most animals in
a children's zoo
are tame and gentle.

Scottish Sheep

Learning about animals

Biologists, zoologists, and naturalists are scientists who study living things. They often work in laboratories or even in their own homes. But sometimes they go to wild parts of the world to study the animals living there.

The things these scientists learn help us know more about the world around us.

Rhesus Monkey

This zoology student is studying animals in the mountains of India. The rhesus monkey seems to be studying the student.

Canada Geese

This biologist is putting numbered bands on the necks of Canada geese. This will help scientists study the geese after they are turned loose.

Roger Tory Peterson is an artist and photographer who studies birds. He is recording the sounds of king penguins.

King Penguins

Jacques Cousteau has spent his life exploring beneath the ocean. He makes movies of the fish and animals that live in the water.

Jacques Cousteau's crew is taking pictures deep in the ocean. They are 60 feet deep.

Learning from animals

Some animals are a lot like people. They can be happy or sad or angry. They can be brave or afraid. They can learn things and solve easy problems.

Scientists called psychologists often study these animals to learn why they act as they do. And sometimes this helps the psychologists understand why people act as they do. By studying the animals, psychologists learn more about people.

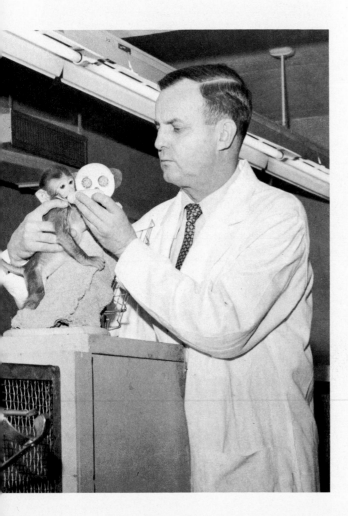

The things Dr. Harry Harlow has learned about baby monkeys may help us find better ways of raising human babies.

Rhesus Monkey

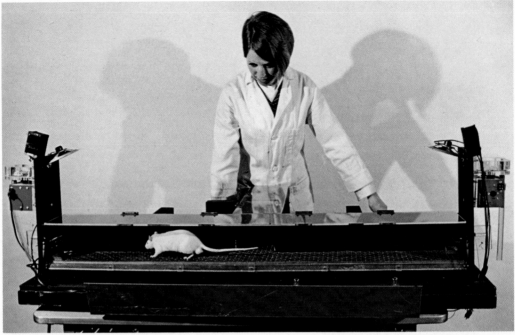

White Rat

This psychologist is trying different ways of helping the rat learn things. Maybe one of the ways will help humans, too.

Dr. Konrad Lorenz has spent his life studying animals and making friends with them. He has written many interesting books.

Geese

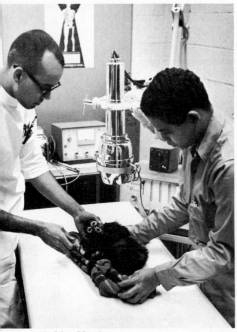

Spider Monkey

Veterinarians take as much
care of their animal patients
as doctors do of people.

Taking care of animals

Veterinarians, game wardens, and forest rangers are people whose work is to care for animals.

Veterinarians are animal doctors. They are as well trained as the doctors that take care of people.

Game wardens and rangers help protect the wild animals in national parks and game preserves.

Kongoni

Veterinarians do important work by
helping to keep whole herds of
animals from getting sick.

The steenbok was trapped by a flood in
Africa. The ranger went to its rescue
and brought it to dry land.

Steenbok

Alligator

The game warden is going to put a tag
on the alligator. Animals are tagged
so they can be counted easily.

White Rats

These rats aren't being hurt. The
machines around them are finding out
what air pollution—dirty air—has
done to the rats' bodies. This can
help us learn what pollution does to
people, because things that are harmful to animals often harm people, too.

Getting help from animals

Animals help scientists who look for ways to keep people well. Some kinds of animals get the same diseases people do. So if a scientist can learn how to make an animal well, he may learn how to make people well, too. By working with animals, scientists have discovered many kinds of medicine that help people.

From his work with animals, Dr. Min Chueh Chang has found medicines that help people.

Dr. Albert Szent-Gyorgyi is a biochemist. By working with animals he has discovered much about how people's bodies work.

Making pictures of animals

It must be lots of fun to be an animal artist or photographer. These people go everywhere in the world to take and make pictures of different kinds of animals. Their pictures are used in books like this one. They also are used in magazines; by zoos, museums, and libraries; and as decorations in people's homes.

Artist Don Eckelberry spends many hours in the woods looking at the kinds of birds he wants to paint. He makes quick drawings of as many as he sees. Then, with the drawings to help him, he goes back to his studio and begins the painting.

This painting of bobwhites is
by animal artist Don Eckelberry.

Domestic Animals

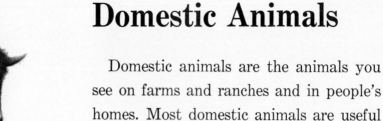

The Tibetan yak is a domestic animal.

Domestic animals are the animals you see on farms and ranches and in people's homes. Most domestic animals are useful to people in some way.

From some domestic animals we get food—meat, milk, eggs, butter, and cheese.

We get leather and cloth from the skins and hair of some domestic animals.

Some domestic animals do work for people, by carrying heavy loads and pulling carts and wagons.

Some kinds of glue, soap, cooking shortening, and other things are made from the bodies of domestic animals.

Some domestic animals help us have fun. We ride on them or watch them race or do tricks.

And some domestic animals are pets that give us friendship and love.

The Indian elephant is a domestic animal.

The Angora goat is a domestic animal. ▶

The chicken is a domestic animal.

Meat and milk

Cattle are important domestic animals. From beef cattle we get steaks, roast beef, and hamburgers. From dairy cattle we get milk for drinking and for making into cream, butter, cheese, and ice cream.

Most of the leather used for shoes comes from the skin of cattle.

Cattle are raised for milk or meat nearly everywhere in the world.

Milk cows, such as these, are called dairy cattle. Many farms in many parts of the world have small herds of dairy cattle.

Dairy Cattle

Beef Cattle

Steaks, roast beef, and hamburgers
come from beef cattle such as
these. Beef cattle are usually
kept in large herds.

Tom Turkey

Many people have turkey for dinner on
Thanksgiving Day in the United States.

Chickens are raised on farms
for their eggs and meat.

White Rock Hen

Meat and eggs

Do you like scrambled eggs, fried chicken, roast duck? These foods come from birds that are raised on farms. Birds that are raised for food are called poultry. Chickens, ducks, geese, and turkeys are the most important kind of poultry.

Most farms raise some poultry. But some farms raise nothing but poultry. And, of course, these are called poultry farms.

Long Island Ducks

Chickens and turkeys have white meat and dark meat. But all the meat on a duck is dark.

Roast goose is a favorite Christmas dinner in England and some other countries.

Geese

This sheep is ready to be
sheared. Its wool coat is
thick and heavy.

The wool is carefully sheared
off in one piece. This
doesn't hurt the sheep.

Sheep

These sheep have had their wool sheared
off. The wool will soon begin to grow again.

Meat and cloth

Sheep are important. Clothes, blankets, and many other things are made from their wool.

There are big herds of sheep on farms in many parts of the world. Once or twice a year, all the sheep are sheared. Their wool is cut off and sent to factories where it is made into cloth.

We get food from sheep, too. Leg of lamb, lamb chops, and mutton come from sheep.

Angora rabbit fur can be made into clothes, too.

Angora Rabbit

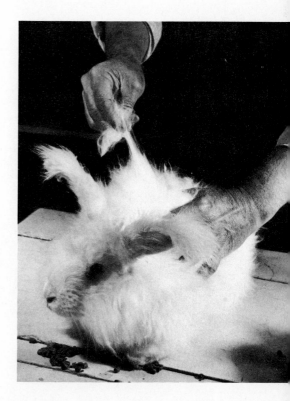

Meat and much more

Someone once said that people can use every part of a hog but its squeal. That's nearly true. From hogs we get ham, bacon, pork chops, roast pork, sausages, spare ribs —even pickled pig's feet. The skin of hogs is made into gloves, shoes, and belts. Hog fat is made into lard, soap, and shaving cream. Hog hair is used in brushes, and ground hog bones are made into glue.

These hogs won a prize in a contest.
One reason they won was that they have
lots of meat and not much fat.

Prize Hogs

Lots of bacon comes from this kind of hog.

Yorkshire Hog

An adult female hog is a sow. A baby hog, less than ten weeks old, is called a pig.

Sow and Pigs

Thoroughbred Horse

Thoroughbreds are slim, handsome horses that can run fast. They are raised for riding and jumping.

Work and play

Horses have been useful to people for thousands of years. People used to do much of their traveling by riding on horses or in carriages that horses pulled. Horses pulled plows and wagons on farms.

Today, machines do most of the work that horses once did. But horses are still raised for riding, racing, and other sports. And in some parts of the world, horses still do a lot of work, too.

In Turkestan, horses are trained for a game called Buzkashi. They must be able to stop, turn, and kneel, quickly.

Bactrian Stallions

Big, strong horses are raised
to pull heavy wagons such as
those in circus parades.

Clydesdale Horses

Special helpers

Dogs make good pets. They make good helpers, too. They are smart and easy to train, so they are often trained to do special jobs.

Pilot Guide Dog

Guide dogs help blind people walk without stumbling or bumping into things.

Sheep dogs are trained to help take care of herds of sheep.

Sheep Dog

In some cold, snowy parts of
the world, people
travel on big sleds that dogs
are trained to pull.

Sled Dogs

When these dogs smell a bird
or animal, they point their
noses at it to show their
master where it is.

Hunting Dogs

Household pets

A pet is an animal friend that lives with you. It may be a big, friendly St. Bernard dog that licks your nose each morning to wake you up. Or maybe it's a fat little hamster that squeaks at you whenever you pass its cage. Whatever it is, remember that it's up to you to give it the care it needs! That's the most important part of owning a pet.

Give a dog or cat food and fresh water each day. Give it a warm, clean place to sleep. Most of all, give it love!

Dog and Cat

Parakeets

Clean your parakeet's cage
each day and give it fresh seeds
and water. It likes green, leafy
vegetables, too.

Goldfish

A goldfish doesn't need much
care. Just keep its water clean
and feed it a tiny bit of fish food
or breadcrumbs once a day.

Hamster

A hamster is clean and friendly.
It will eat stale bread, nuts, fruit,
and vegetables. Its cage should
be kept out of bright light.

Gerbil

Frisky little animals need
exercise. If a mouse or gerbil
has a wheel like this in its cage,
it can run as much as it likes.

In other lands

Many animals we see in zoos are domestic animals of far-off lands.

In India and Southeast Asia, elephants help build roads and clear forests. Camels pull plows and carry people in parts of Africa and Asia. In many parts of the world people keep herds of goats, yaks, camels, llamas, and even reindeer, just as other farmers keep herds of cows or sheep.

In Lapland and parts of Russia, teams of reindeer are trained to pull loads.

Reindeer

Cow and Calf

Llamas

In some parts of India, cows live right in their owners' houses. They are kept for milk but never for meat. In South America, many people use llamas for food, clothing, and to carry things. In African and Asian countries, donkeys and camels are used for riding and for carrying things.

Donkey and Camel

Vanishing Animals

You have never seen one of the big, funny-looking birds called dodos. They are extinct. That means there aren't any dodos alive anymore. But 300 years ago, there were many thousands of dodos.

Today, there are many thousands of polar bears, rhinoceroses, and tigers. But they, and many other animals, may soon be extinct, too! Many animals are vanishing. Some are being killed by dirty air and water. Some are being killed by too much hunting. Some are dying because they have no room.

Many persons are doing everything they can to keep animals from becoming extinct. But if these people aren't able to save the animals, many of our favorite kinds of animals may soon vanish forever—just like the dodos.

The great auk is extinct.

The dodo is extinct. ▶

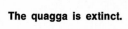

The quagga is extinct.

People are killing many animals

Almost everywhere in the world more and more wild animals are being killed by people. Many animals are killed for their skins or feathers or horns or tusks. Many animals die when the land where they find their food is covered by factories or airports or highways. Some animals are killed by accident. But unless the killing stops, many kinds of animals will soon be gone from the earth.

These are the skulls of rhinoceroses that were killed just so their horns could be cut off. The horns are sold to people who think they are medicine.

Rhinoceros Skulls

These tusks and skins were taken from hunters who had broken the law by killing too many animals. The hunters wanted to sell the tusks and skins.

Elephant Tusks and Leopard Skins

Many walruses are killed for their tusks. Eskimos carve the tusks into toys to sell. But too many walruses have been killed, so now there are laws to protect them.

Walrus

The green sea turtles may soon all be gone. They are killed for soup, for oil, and for their skins.

Green Sea Turtle

Potomac River Fish

Fish take water into their gills to
breathe. If too much waste material is
in the water, the fish are killed.

Dirty air and water kill animals

Animals need clean air and water. Many animals cannot breathe air that has lots of smoke and soot in it. Fish and other animals can't live in lakes and rivers that have lots of garbage and waste materials in them. When oil covers the waters of the ocean, many sea animals and birds are killed. And insect sprays kill other animals besides insects.

Water birds can't tell when there is oil in the water. When they try to swim in the oily water, they drown.

Oil Soaked Cormorant

Helping to save animals

Many people work to help keep animals from being killed. For some people, such as game wardens and rangers, helping animals is part of their job. Other people do what they can just because they like animals—and want to save them.

Ducks

Ducks can't find food when rivers and ponds are frozen. These men are breaking the ice so the ducks won't starve.

Hundreds of sea birds were trapped in oily water in the ocean near California. People worked to save as many as they could.

Cleaning Water Birds

White-Tailed Deer

This deer was trapped by a flood. The
game wardens put it to sleep with
drugs and took it to safety.

Giraffe

There wasn't enough food where this
giraffe lived. It would have starved.
But men caught it and moved it by
truck to a place where there was
plenty of food. Whole herds of animals
have been saved this way.

Zoos save some kinds of
animals by bringing males
and females, such as these
oryxes, together. There
aren't many of these oryxes
left. But if these two have
babies and the babies grow up
and have more babies, there
will soon be more oryxes than
there are now. They will be
saved from becoming extinct.

Arabian Oryxes

Lions in Nairobi National Park

In some parts of the world, places
where many animals live together have
been made into big parks. The animals
are free, but people can come to see them
as the people in the picture are doing.
And the animals are safe—people
may not come into the parks to hunt.

Favorite animals

Do you know what your favorite animals eat, or how big they are? Now you can find out. As you read about each animal's size remember that a four-footed animal's height is measured from its shoulder to its foot. Its length is from its nose to the end of its tail.

Aardvark. The aardvark lives in Africa. It has a nose like a pig, ears like a donkey, and sharp claws on its feet. It uses its claws to tear open termite nests so it can lick up the termites with its long, sticky tongue. The aardvark is 4 to 6 feet long.

Alpaca. The alpaca is about 4 feet tall. It looks like a tiny camel in a big, shaggy coat. In the mountains of South America, where alpacas live, people make clothes and blankets of alpaca wool. Alpacas are tame and are kept in herds.

Anteater. The giant anteater lives on the grassy plains of South America. It is about 6 feet long, and its body is greyish-brown with a black-and-white mark on the throat and back. Anteaters break into termite nests and lick up the termites with their long, sticky tongues.

Armadillo. The nine-banded armadillo lives in the Southern United States, Mexico, and South America. It is about 2 feet long. When it is frightened, it curls up into a ball and its bony armor protects it. Armadillos hunt for their food at night. They eat worms and insects.

Baboon. The baboon looks cross and fierce—and it is! Large groups of baboons live together on the plains of Africa. They eat lizards, insects, and roots. Sometimes they wander onto farms and eat any food they can find. A baboon is about 3 feet tall as it walks on hands and feet.

Badger. Badgers live in many parts of the world. European and Asian badgers are about 3 feet long. American badgers are smaller. The badger eats rabbits, snakes, rats, and insects. It is a good fighter. If a bigger animal picks a fight with a badger, the badger nearly always wins.

Bat. The bat is the only mammal that can fly. During the day bats sleep in caves or other dark places. At night they go out to eat. Most bats eat insects that they catch as they fly. Some bats eat fruit. Most bats are a few inches long.

Bear. The Alaskan brown bear is the biggest meat-eating land animal. It is about 9 feet long. The black bear, which lives in North America and Mexico, is about 5 feet long. Most bears eat fruit, nuts, fish, insects, and small animals. All bears can be dangerous—even tame ones!

Beaver. The beaver lives along streams in North America and northern Europe and Asia. It eats tree bark and water plants and can chew down small, slim trees to make a dam. The beaver is about 3 or 4 feet long. It has a wide, flat tail.

Boa Constrictor. There are many kinds of boas, but they all get their food the same way. The boa wraps itself around an animal and squeezes. The animal can't breathe, and it dies. Then the boa swallows the animal. A boa may be 10 to 14 feet long. It eats rats, birds, and other small animals.

Bobcat. The bobcat is a short-tailed wildcat that lives in the woods and swamps of North America and Mexico. It can see well in the dark and does most of its hunting at night. It eats rabbits, squirrels, and even deer and wild turkeys. A bobcat is about 15 inches high.

Buffalo. This animal's real name is American bison. The bison is about 6 feet tall and 12 feet long. It eats grass. Once there were millions of bison. Today there are only a few small herds in Wyoming and Colorado; and in Alberta, Canada.

Buffalo. Big herds of cape buffalo live in South and East Africa. The cape buffalo is about 5 feet tall. Its horns are long and sharp. If a cape buffalo becomes angry it charges—and almost nothing can stop it! A cape buffalo eats grass.

Bush Baby. The bush baby lives in the hot forests of Africa. It moves through the trees by jumping from one branch to another. Some bush babies are as big as cats, others are as small as mice. A bush baby eats grasshoppers, fruits, seeds, and flowers. It is also called a galago.

Camel. The Arabian camel has one hump. It lives in the hot, sandy deserts of Arabia and North Africa. The Bactrian camel has two humps. It lives on the rocky deserts and snowy plains of central Asia. Most camels are about 7 feet tall. Camels eat dates, grain, and dried grass.

Cheetah. The cheetah is a big, spotted cat that lives on grassy plains in Africa and parts of Asia. It is 3 to 4 feet high. Cheetahs are the fastest runners of all the animals. They get their food by chasing gazelles, impalas, and other animals.

Chimpanzee. Chimpanzees live together in little groups in the forests of western Africa. The group moves through the forest looking for nuts, fruits, and berries. Some full-grown chimpanzees are nearly as tall as a small man. Chimpanzees are the smartest of all the apes.

Chipmunk. The chipmunk looks like a striped squirrel with a short tail. It lives in underground tunnels where it keeps piles of nuts, seeds, and dried fruit and berries. Chipmunks live in North America and northern Asia.

Crocodile. The crocodile lives in swamps and on riverbanks in many hot parts of the world. It is the largest and heaviest of all living reptiles. Some crocodiles are more than 20 feet long. A crocodile will eat any animal it can catch—even a man. Alligators are crocodiles' cousins.

Deer. Deer are the only animals that have branched horns called antlers. Red deer, white-tailed deer, reindeer, elk, and caribou are some of the many kinds of deer. The pudu, the smallest deer, is about a foot high. The North American moose, the biggest deer, is 6 or 7 feet high. Deer eat grass and plants.

Dingo. The dingo is a wild dog that lives in packs in Australia. It is about the size of a collie. Most dingoes are yellowish-brown color. They eat small kangaroos and other small animals. Dingo puppies make good pets.

Dolphin. The dolphin looks like a fish but it is really a mammal like a dog or cat or horse. Dolphins can't breathe in water as fish do, but must breathe air. Dolphins live in the warmest parts of the ocean. They swim in small groups, hunting for fish. Common dolphins are 6 feet long.

Duckbill (Platypus). The platypus is a mammal like a dog or a cat. But it has a bill like a duck's and it lays eggs like a bird's or reptile's! The platypus is about 24 inches long. It lives near rivers in Australia. It eats shrimps, worms, and tadpoles.

Elephant. Elephants live in Africa and southern Asia. The African elephant is the biggest of all land animals. The biggest African elephants are about 13 feet tall. Elephants live together in small herds. They eat leaves.

Fox. The little red fox lives in North America, Europe, Asia, and North Africa. During the day it stays in its den. At night it goes out to hunt squirrels, mice, insects, and small animals. Foxes belong to the dog family.

Gazelle. Different kinds of gazelles live in small groups in Africa, India, Asia Minor, and Mongolia. Most gazelles are about 2 or 3 feet tall and can run faster than racehorses. They eat grass.

Giraffe. The giraffe's neck is longer than your whole body. But the giraffe has no more bones in its neck than you have in your neck. The bones in its neck are just longer. Giraffes live on the grassy plains of Africa. They eat leaves and twigs of acacia trees. A newborn baby giraffe is as tall as a tall man. And a grown-up giraffe is three times taller!

Gnu. The gnu looks big and clumsy, but it is one of the fastest of all animals. It is about as big as a pony. It spends its mornings and evenings eating grass and drinking water. During the day it sleeps. Gnus live in big herds on the plains of Africa.

Goldfish. Goldfish are kept as pets in glass bowls and ponds. There are red, orange, brown, white, and even black goldfish! Some goldfish are a few inches long and some are more than a foot long. Goldfish eat worms, tiny insects, breadcrumbs, and bits of plants.

Gorilla. The gorilla lives in Africa. Families of gorillas move through the forests eating young plants and fruit. Some gorillas are as tall as a tall man. Gorillas are very strong, but they are not dangerous unless they are bothered.

Hamster. The wild hamster lives in an underground tunnel and sleeps during the day. At night it hunts for seeds and fruit that it stores in its tunnels. Wild hamsters live in eastern Europe and western Asia. Tame hamsters, sold by pet shops, are called golden hamsters. They are about 5 inches long.

Hippopotamus. The hippopotamus lives in swamps and rivers in the hottest parts of Africa. A big hippopotamus may be 5 feet tall and 14 feet long and weigh 2 tons. It can open its mouth 4 feet wide! The hippopotamus eats grass and water plants.

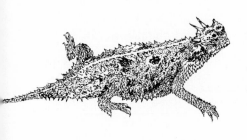

Horned Toad. The horned toad is really a lizard. It lives in deserts and dry places in Mexico and the Western United States. A horned toad is about 3 inches long and eats insects and spiders. It squirts a stream of blood from its eye if it is bothered!

Impala. Big herds of impala live in open country in South and East Africa. The impala eats leaves and grass. When it sees or smells danger the impala makes a noise like a sneeze. Then all the other impalas go leaping away. The impala is about 3 feet tall.

Jerboa. Most jerboas live in deserts in Africa, Arabia, and southwest Asia. During the hot day the jerboa sleeps in an underground hole. In the cool night the jerboa goes out to hunt for seeds and insects. The jerboa is about 15 inches long. It hops like a kangaroo and can walk on two legs.

Kangaroo. Kangaroos live in Australia and on nearby islands. The mothers carry their babies in pouches like pockets on their stomachs. The baby is only an inch long when it's born. But a full-grown kangaroo may be 7 feet tall and can jump 25 feet! A kangaroo eats plants.

Koala. The koala eats only eucalyptus leaves and spends most of its life in eucalyptus trees. Mother koalas have pouches like kangaroos. Baby koalas stay in the pouches for 6 months, then they ride on their mothers' backs. The koala is about 2 feet long. It lives in Australia.

Komodo Dragon Lizard. The Komodo dragon lizard is the biggest of the lizards. It may grow to be 10 feet long. It lives on the island of Komodo and a few other islands in Southeast Asia. It eats small live or dead animals.

Leopard. Leopards live by themselves in the jungles of Africa and Asia. They sometimes hide in trees and jump onto deer and other animals that pass beneath them. The leopard is about 7 feet long. A leopard with an all-black body is called a black panther.

Lion. Lions are the only cats that like to live in groups. Most lions live in Africa but there are a few in India. A full-grown lion is about 9 feet long and 3 feet tall. A lion will hunt and eat any large animal except an elephant, rhinoceros, or hippopotamus. Female lions do most of the hunting.

Mole. The mole spends nearly all its life underground. Each day it digs tunnels to find worms and grubs to eat. The mole can hardly see at all, but it hears and smells very well. The most common kind of mole is about 8 inches long. Moles live in North America, Africa, Europe and Asia.

Mouse. Mice live in meadows, forests, deserts, and houses almost everywhere in the world. Most mice eat seeds, grain, fruit, and nuts. But some mice eat insects and some even eat other mice! Most mice are just a few inches long.

Musk Ox. The shaggy musk ox lives far north in Alaska, Canada, and Greenland. It scrapes snow with its hoofs to find the moss and twigs it eats. Musk oxen live together in herds. The musk ox is about 7 feet long and 4 feet tall.

Octopus. The octopus has a round body, bulgy eyes, and eight arms called tentacles. Its mouth is like a parrot's bill. The octopus catches lobsters and other water animals with its tentacles and tears them apart with its bill. Most octopus' bodies are about the size of a man's fist.

Orang-Utan. Orang-utans live in small groups in jungles on the islands of Borneo and Sumatra. They move by swinging from one tree branch to another with their arms. The orang-utan is 3 to 5 feet tall. It eats fruit, flowers, leaves, and insects.

Ostrich. The ostrich is the biggest of all birds, but it can't fly. Its wings are too small. But an ostrich can run faster than a racehorse! Ostriches live in deserts in Africa. They eat plants that grow in the desert, and sometimes lizards.

Otter. Many kinds of otters live near rivers and lakes nearly everywhere in the world. One kind of otter spends most of its life in the sea. Sea otters eat fish, crabs, and clams. River otters eat fish, crayfish, frogs, and turtles. River otters are about 4 feet long.

Owl. Owls live almost everywhere in the world in forests, deserts, meadows, and barns. Most owls sleep during the day. At night they hunt such animals as mice, rabbits, rats, fish, frogs, insects, and worms. They can fly without making a sound. There are many different kinds of owls.

Panda. The giant panda looks like a black-and-white bear. But many scientists think that pandas are really big raccoons. The giant panda lives in the mountains in Southern China. It eats young bamboo plants. A giant panda is about 6 feet long and 3 feet tall.

Pelican. The pelican lives in many parts of the world. It's a champion fisherman. It dives into water with its bill open. The pouch under its bill stretches out and scoops up water and fish. The pelican dumps out the water and eats the fish. A pelican is about 5 feet long.

Penguin. The penguin is a bird that can't fly. But it's a wonderful swimmer. All penguins live in the southern part of the world. Some even live right on the ice near the South Pole. The biggest penguin is 4 feet tall and the smallest is about a foot tall. Penguins eat fish and some shellfish.

Piranha. Piranhas usually swim in large groups. They are more dangerous than sharks. They will rush at any animal that comes into the water and eat it alive, leaving nothing but bones. Piranhas live in rivers in South America. A piranha is from 4 to 18 inches long.

Porcupine. The porcupine is well protected by sharp stickers, called quills, all over its body. American porcupines are good tree climbers, but other porcupines can't climb. The porcupine is about 3 feet long. It eats bark and roots.

Pygmy Marmoset. The pygmy marmoset is the smallest of all monkeys. Its body is only 4 inches long. The pygmy marmoset lives in the hot Amazon forest of South America. It scampers about in the trees hunting for nuts, fruit, and insects to eat.

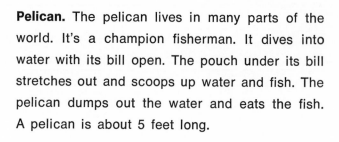

Rabbit. The cottontail rabbit lives in prairies and meadows in North and South America. In the summer it eats green plants. In the winter it eats twigs and bark. European rabbits are much like cottontails, but they dig tunnels in which to live. The cottontail rabbit is from 8 to 14 inches long.

Raccoon. The raccoon lives in hollow trees and caves in the forests of North and South America. It uses its paws like little hands, to catch things in water and to put food into its mouth. The raccoon is about 32 inches long. It eats frogs, turtles, snails, insects, corn, and fruit.

Rat. Rats live nearly everywhere in the world. The black rat and brown rat eat almost anything and destroy much food. They also carry diseases. The black rat's body is about 8 inches long. Its thin tail is longer than its body.

Rattlesnake. Rattlesnakes live in many parts of North and South America. They have bony rattles on their tails that make buzzing noises when the snakes shake them. A rattlesnake kills small animals with poison, then it swallows them whole. A diamondback rattlesnake is about 7 feet long.

Reindeer. Large herds of reindeer live in the cold, far northern parts of the world. The reindeer has a thick fur coat and broad, round hoofs that help it walk on snow. It eats grass in the summer and moss in winter. A reindeer is about 3½ feet tall.

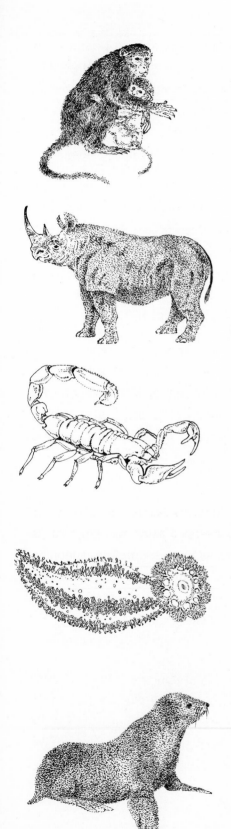

Rhesus Monkey. Rhesus monkeys live in large groups in forests and on rocky hillsides in southern Asia. They are clever and active. They eat leaves and fruit and often rob fruit from gardens and orchards. A rhesus monkey is about 2 feet tall.

Rhinoceros. Different kinds of rhinoceroses live in Africa and parts of Asia. A rhinoceros eats grass, twigs, and leaves of bushes. It spends much of its time lying in soft, wet mud. A white rhinoceros is about 5 feet 8 inches tall.

Scorpion. Scorpions live in deserts and jungles in many hot parts of the world. A scorpion hides during the day and comes out at night to hunt. It catches insects and spiders with its claws and poisons them with the sting in its tail. The biggest scorpions are about 8 inches long.

Sea Cucumber. This strange animal lives on the bottom of the ocean. At one end of its body is a little mouth. Around the mouth are many arms like bunches of leaves. The sea cucumber pulls tiny plants and animals into its mouth with its arms. Most sea cucumbers are about a foot long.

Seal. Most kinds of seals live in herds in the oceans, along coasts of land. A seal must breathe air but it can stay under water for as long as 20 minutes. Seals eat fish, squids, and sea birds. A male elephant seal is about 21 feet long. A ringed seal is about 4 feet long.

Shark. The shark is a big fish that usually lives in warm parts of the ocean. It eats smaller fish and almost anything else it can get—even people! The biggest shark is about 50 feet long. It eats only small fish and plants.

Skunk. The skunk lives in North and South America. It defends itself by shooting a bad-smelling liquid from a place near its tail. Other animals can't stand the smell and leave skunks alone. The skunk is about the size of a cat. It eats leaves, insects, fruit, nuts, and mice and other small animals.

Sloth. The sloth lives in hot jungles in South America. It spends most of its life hanging upside down in trees. It moves slowly along each branch, eating leaves and twigs. It hardly ever comes down except to climb another tree. The sloth is about 2 feet long.

Snapping Turtle. Most turtles are timid but the snapping turtle is fierce. It bites so hard that its strong jaws make a loud snap! The snapping turtle lives in North America and often grows to be more than 2 feet long. It eats fish, insects, crayfish, and water plants.

Spider. Spiders live almost everywhere. They have eight legs and most of them have eight eyes, too. Most spiders eat insects they catch in webs or by hunting. Some of the biggest tarantula spiders often eat small birds, lizards, and mice.

Spider Monkey. These monkeys live in little groups in Central American jungles. The spider monkey's body is about 2 feet long and its tail is longer than its body. The monkey uses its tail like an extra hand as it swings through the trees. The spider monkey eats insects, fruit, flowers, and nuts.

Spitting Cobra. This snake can shoot a stream of poison several feet into the eyes of an animal or a person. The poison kills small animals and can make a person blind. Most spitting cobras are about 5 feet long. They eat small animals. Spitting cobras live in Africa.

Squirrel. The squirrel lives in many parts of the world. It eats nuts, fruits, seeds, and insects. In the fall, squirrels find all the food they can and store it up for winter. The gray squirrel is about 2 feet long from its nose to the end of its tail.

Swordfish. The swordfish lives in warm parts of the ocean. It swims into groups of small fish and kills as many as it can with the sharp, bony sword on its nose. Then it eats all the fish it has killed. The swordfish is about 7 feet long.

Tapir. The tapir lives in hot jungles in South America, Malaya, and Sumatra. It has four toes on its front feet, but only three toes on its back feet. The South American tapir is about 6 feet long and 3 feet tall. It eats plants and fruit.

Tarsier. The tarsier lives in trees in the East Indies and Philippines. It is a great jumper and catches insects and lizards by jumping at them and catching them with its hands. The tarsier's body is about 6 inches long.

Tasmanian Devil. The Tasmanian devil lives on the island of Tasmania, near Australia. It is about 3 feet long and is a fierce hunter. It eats small kangaroos, lizards, birds, and sometimes even sheep. Mother Tasmanian devils, like mother kangaroos, have pouches.

Tiger. Tigers live in many parts of Asia, in the hot, southern jungles as well as the cold, snowy, northern forests. The tiger likes to live and hunt by itself. It eats deer, antelope, wild cattle, and even young elephants. Most tigers' bodies are about 9 or 10 feet long.

Tortoise. Tortoises are land turtles. And the biggest of all land turtles lives on the Galapagos Islands near Central America. The Galapagos tortoise is so big that a child can easily ride on its back. It eats grass, fruit, and plants. Some of these tortoises are over 100 years old.

Vampire Bat. Yes, there really is a vampire bat! But it doesn't really suck blood. It cuts sleeping animals with its sharp teeth and licks their blood with its tongue. The vampire bat is only about 3 inches long. It lives in South and Central America.

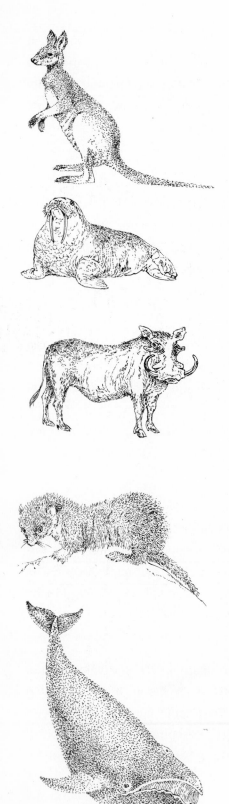

Wallaby. The wallaby belongs to the kangaroo family. It looks like a small, fat kangaroo with short legs. The mother wallaby keeps her baby in a pouch just as a mother kangaroo does. The wallaby eats leaves and plants. It lives in Australia.

Walrus. Walruses live together in herds in the cold water and on the floating ice near the North Pole. A walrus eats mainly clams and shellfish that it digs out of the sandy sea-bottom with its long tusks. A full-grown male walrus is about 12 feet long.

Wart Hog. The wart hog gets it name from the bumpy warts on its face. Wart hogs live in small groups in sandy places in Africa. They eat grass, roots, and sometimes small animals. The wart hog is about 30 inches tall.

Weasel. The weasel lives almost everywhere in the world. It can move quickly and get in and out of tight places when it hunts. It eats only meat—rats, mice, frogs, lizards, and birds. The most common weasel is about 16 inches long.

Whale. Whales live almost everywhere in the ocean. The whale looks like a big fish but it's really a mammal, like a dog or cat, and must breathe air. The toothed whale eats fish and other water animals. The baleen whale eats tiny plants and animals that it strains out of the water. All whales are huge, but the biggest of all is the blue whale. The biggest blue whales are about 100 feet long.

Wolf. Wolves live in Europe, Asia, and North America. They usually travel and hunt together in small groups called packs. The big timber wolf eats deer, moose, and smaller animals. A smaller wolf, such as the red wolf, eats rabbits and other small animals. A timber wolf is about 3 feet tall.

Wolverine. The wolverine lives in the northern parts of North America, Europe, and Asia. It is a strong, fierce fighter. It eats rabbits and other small animals and sometimes even reindeer. The wolverine likes to live and hunt by itself. It is about 2 or 3 feet long.

Wombat. The wombat lives in Australia and Tasmania. It is a digger and lives in underground tunnels during the day. At night it comes out to eat grass, bark, and roots. A mother wombat, like a mother kangaroo, has a pouch to keep her baby in. The wombat is about 3 feet long.

Yak. The yak belongs to the cow family. It lives in the high parts of Tibet. There are herds of wild yaks, but the Tibetan people keep herds of tame yaks, too. A wild yak is about 6 feet tall. A tame yak is a little smaller. Yaks eat grass.

Zebra. Most zebras live on grassy plains in Africa. They move about in herds, eating grass. All zebras look like striped horses, but different kinds of zebras have different kinds of stripes. The zebra is 4 or 5 feet tall.

Hard Words

Aardvark (AHRD vAHRK)

An African mammal with a piglike snout, a long, sticky tongue, long claws, and a long tail.

Ajolote (ah-hoh-LOH-tey)

A two-legged lizard with a wormlike body.

Algae (AL jee)

Plants that live mainly in water and make their own food.

Ameba (uh MEE buh)

A tiny animal that can be seen only with a microscope.

Amphibian (am FIB ee un)

An animal that lives in water and breathes with gills when it is a baby. It lives on land and breathes with lungs when it is an adult. Frogs and toads are amphibians.

Anaconda (AN uh KAHN duh)

A large snake that lives near water and eats mainly birds and small animals. It lives in South America.

Anglaspis (an GLAS pihs)

A jawless, fishlike animal that lived in the sea millions of years ago.

Aphid (AY fihd)

A tiny insect that feeds by sucking juice from plants and trees.

Arachnid (uh RAK nihd)

An insectlike animal with no feelers or wings. It has four pairs of jointed legs. Spiders and daddy-longlegs are arachnids.

Archaeopteryx
  (AHR kee AHP tur ihks)

A crow-sized bird with claws on its wings, and teeth. It lived millions of years ago.

Armadillo (AHR muh DIHL oh)

A small animal with bits of bone fitted close together over its body to protect it from its enemies.

Arthropod (AHR throh pod)

An animal with many jointed legs and a shell covering that may be thick and strong or thin and weak. Insects, spiders, and shrimps are arthropods.

Bacteria (back TEE rih uh)

Tiny creatures that can be seen only with a microscope. They may be oval, rod-shaped, or spiral.

Biochemist (by oh KEHM ihst)

A person who studies the life changes in plants, animals, and humans.

Biologist (by AHL uh jihst)

A person who studies living things.

Birkenia (buhr KEE nee uh)

A small, fishlike animal that lived in the sea millions of years ago.

Bombardier beetle
(bom buhr DEER)

A ground beetle that makes a popping sound and lets off a reddish-colored, bad-smelling steam when it is in danger.

Brachiopod (BRACK ee uh pahd)

A shellfish with two shells that are shaped differently from each other.

Brachiosaurus
(BRACK ee uh SAWR uhs)

One of the largest of all dinosaurs. It had a huge body and a short tail.

Brontosaurus
(BRAHN tuh SAWR uhs)

A gigantic, plant-eating dinosaur with four elephantlike legs, a long neck, and a long tail.

Caecilian (see sill EE uhn)

An animal that looks somewhat like a worm but is related to frogs and toads.

Centipede (SEN tuh peed)

A small, wormlike animal whose body is divided into many parts, each of which has a pair of thin legs attached.

Cephalaspis
(sef uh LASS pihs)

A kind of fish that lived millions of years ago. It had a large bony shield attached to its head.

Chaffinch (CHAFF inch)

A small European songbird with a strong, cone-shaped bill for cracking seeds.

Chameleon (kuh MEE lee un)

A lizard that can change colors.

Cicada (sih KAY dah)

An insect with four thin wings. The male cicada makes a buzzing sound.

Coccosteus
(KUH kah steh uhs)

A fishlike animal that lived in the sea millions of years ago.

Cocoon (kuh COON)

The silky covering that some caterpillars spin before they change into butterflies.

Coelophysis (see LAHF ih siss)

One of the first dinosaurs. It had a long neck and a long tail. It ran on its hind legs.

Conch (kahngk)

A large, heavy, sea snail that has a twisty, cone-shaped shell.

Copepod (KOH puh pahd)

A tiny, shrimplike animal that lives in both fresh and salt water.

Crustacean (crus TAY shun)

An animal with a shell-covered body and many jointed legs. It lives in the water. Crabs, lobsters, shrimps, and crayfish are crustaceans.

Diatom (DY uh tahm)

A tiny water plant.

Dimetrodon
(dy MEH truh don)

A reptile with a large fin on its back. The dimetrodon lived millions of years ago.

Dinosaur (DY nuh sawr)

A reptile that lived millions of years ago.

Dolphin (DAHL fin)

A sea mammal that belongs to the whale family but is smaller than a whale.

Echidna (ee KID nuh)

A small mammal with a flattened body covered with coarse hair and sharp growths called spines.

Elephant-nose mormyrid
(MOHR mih rid)

An African fresh-water fish with a long snout that bends downward like an elephant's trunk.

Eohippus (ee oh HIP uhs)

The ancestor of today's horse. It was as small as a cat. It lived millions of years ago.

Euglena (yu GLEE nuh)

Tiny creatures that can be seen only with a microscope. They live in fresh water.

Euplotes (yu PLOHD eez)

A creature with tiny hairlike growths that push it through the water in which it lives. It can be seen only with a microscope.

Gerbil (JUR bihl)

A furry, mouselike animal with a long tail. It lives in the dry sandy parts of Africa and Asia.

Gnu (noo)

A large African animal with a thick neck, a big head with long, curved horns, skinny legs, and a long tail. It is also known as a wildebeest (WILL duh beest).

Great auk (awk)

A bird that lived on the coasts of the North Atlantic. There are no great auks alive today.

Grebe (greeb)

A diving bird with a flattened body covered with waterproof feathers.

Hedgehog (HEJ hahg)

A small, insect-eating animal with a long nose, short tail, and stiff pointed growths called spines on its back.

Hibernation (hy buhr NAY shun)

A kind of sleep that some animals take during the winter.

Ichthyostega
(ick thee AHS tee guh)

A fish with legs. It lived millions of years ago.

Iguanid (ih GWAH nihd)

A kind of lizard that belongs to the same family as the iguana, the horned toad, and the pine lizard.

Jaguar (JAG wahr)   A large, wild cat with dark yellow fur with black or brown spots.

Jaguarundi (jag wuh RUN dee)   A cat that does not look like a cat. It has a long neck, short, stubby legs, and a long tail.

Jerboa (jur BOH uh)   A tiny, kangaroolike animal that belongs to the same family as mice, rats, and squirrels.

Jewel cichlid (SIK lid)   A small, bright-colored fresh-water fish with spiny fins and jewellike spots of color on its sides.

Kiwi (KEE wee)   A shaggy-feathered bird that cannot fly. It has no tail and no wings. It is about as big as a chicken.

Koala (koh AH luh)   A small Australian animal that looks somewhat like a teddy bear.

Kraken (KRAH kuhn or KRAY kuhn)   An imaginary monster that was said to live in the northern seas, especially near Norway.

Kudu (KOO doo)   A big African antelope that lives in the grassy parts of the Sahara.

Macaw (muh KAW)   A long-tailed parrot.

Millipede (MIL uh peed)   A wormlike animal with many thin legs.

Moeritherium (MEER uh theer ee uhm)   A small animal that lived millions of years ago in Egypt. It is the elephant's ancestor.

Mosquito (muh SKEE toh)   An insect with two wings. Mosquito is the Spanish word for *little fly*.

Naturalist (NACH uhr uh list)   A person who studies plants and animals in the places where they live.

Nuthatch (NUT hach)   A small, climbing bird that lives mostly in trees. It feeds on nuts and insects.

Onychophoran (AHN uh koh FAWR uhn)   A small, wormlike animal with thick, short legs attached to the many parts of its body.

Orang-utan (oh RANG oo tan)   A large ape with long, strong arms.

Oryx (AWR icks)   An African antelope.

Pangolin (pang GO lin)   A mammal that has scales on its body. It looks somewhat like a combination of an anteater and an armadillo.

Paramecium (par uh ME shih um)   A tiny animal that lives in pools and streams. It looks somewhat like a glass slipper. It can be seen only with a microscope.

Platypus (PLAT ih pus)   An egg-laying mammal with a bill like a duck's bill.

Porpoise (PAWR pus)   A small mammal that belongs to the whale family. It is sometimes mistaken for a dolphin.

Protist (PRO tist)   Tiny creatures that sometimes seem to be both plants and animals. They are usually too small to be seen except with a microscope.

Psychologist (sy KAHL uh jist)   A person who examines the reasons why people behave as they do.

Pteranodon (tehr AN uh dahn)   A flying reptile with a body about the size of a turkey's body. It lived millions of years ago.

Pterichthyodes (tuh RIHK thee OH deez)   A kind of fish that lived millions of years ago. Its head and back were protected by a bony armor.

Pterygotus (tehr uh GO tus)   A lobsterlike sea animal about as big as a man. It lived millions of years ago.

Quagga (KWAHG uh)   A South African zebra that had stripes on the front part of its body only. There are no quaggas any more. They are extinct.

Rhamphorhynchus (ram fuh RIN kus)   A flying reptile with a long, paddlelike tail and long, sharp teeth. It lived millions of years ago.

Scallop (SKAHL up)   A shellfish that belongs to the same family as the oyster and the clam.

Sea anemone (uh NEM oh nee)   A bright-colored sea animal that looks like the flower from which it gets its name. It belongs to the same family as the jellyfish and the coral.

Spore (spohr)   A tiny sort of seed. Molds and mushrooms grow from spores.

Stentor (STEN tawhr)   A tiny, trumpet-shaped animal that can be seen only with a microscope.

Sturgeon (STUR jun)   A large fish with a long body.

Stylonurus (sty LAHN uh rus)   A hard-shelled sea animal with many jointed legs. It lived millions of years ago.

Tapir (TAY per)

An animal that looks somewhat like a pig but is related to the horse and the rhinoceros.

Tarsier (TAHR see er)

A small animal with a round head, big, round eyes, big ears, and a long, thin tail. It lives in trees in the East Indies and in the Philippines.

Termite (TUR mite)

An insect that is sometimes called a white ant. Termites live together in nests they dig or build.

Thelodus (thel uh duhs)

A sea animal with tiny toothlike bones covering its body. It lived millions of years ago.

Tortoise (TAWR tus)

A land turtle.

Tremataspis (tree muh TAS pis)

A jawless, bony-armored fish that lived millions of years ago.

Triassochelys (try AHS oh KELL eez)

A turtle that lived millions of years ago. It was much like today's turtles except that it could not pull its head and legs all the way into its shell.

Triceratops (try SEHR uh tops)

A dinosaur that lived in the western part of North America millions of years ago. It had a big head with a horn over each eye and on its nose.

Trilobite (TRY loh bite)

A small sea animal with a pair of legs attached to each of the many parts of its body. It breathed through gills in its legs.

Tuatara (too uh TAH ruh)

A large New Zealand reptile.

Turbot (TUR but)

A large, round, flatfish with both eyes on the left side of its head.

Tyrannosaurus (ty RAN uh SAWR uhs)

A huge, meat-eating dinosaur. It walked upright on its two hind legs. It lived millions of years ago.

Ultraviolet (uhl trah VY oh lit)

A color that some animals can see but that is invisible to people.

Vorticella (VAWR tuh SELL uh)

A tiny creature with a bell-shaped body on a thin stem. It can be seen only with a microscope.

Wrasse (rass)

A spiny-finned, bright-colored fish with thick lips and strong teeth. It lives in warm seas.

Zoologist (zoh AHL oh jihst)

A person who studies animal life.

Zoology (zoh AHL oh jih)

The study of animal life.

Illustration Acknowledgments

The publishers of *Childcraft* gratefully acknowledge the courtesy of the following artists, photographers, publishers, agencies, and corporations for illustrations in this volume. Page numbers refer to two-page spreads. The words "(*left*)," "(*center*)," "(*top*)," "(*bottom*)," and "(*right*)," indicate position on the spread. All illustrations are the exclusive property of the publishers of *Childcraft* unless names are marked with an asterisk (*).

Cover:
- (front) CHILDCRAFT illustrations by Alex Ebel, and Harry McNaught
- (back) CHILDCRAFT illustrations by Guy Tudor, Harry McNaught, Eraldo Carugati, George Lopac, and Walter Linsenmaier

6–7: Eraldo Carugati and George Lopac
8–9: Jane Burton, Bruce Coleman Ltd. (*)
10–11: (*top left*) R. A. Mendez, Photo Trends (*), (*bottom left*) Allan Roberts (*); (*top right*) Nelson Medina, Photo Researchers (*), (*center right*) Warren Garst, Tom Stack & Associates (*), (*bottom right*) Russ Kinne, Photo Researchers (*)
12–13: (*top left*) Appel Color Photography (*), (*bottom left*) Walter Dawn (*); (*top right*) Ralph Buchsbaum (*), (*bottom right*) E. R. Degginger (*)
14–15: (*top left*) Warren Hamilton, U.S. Geological Survey (*), (*bottom left*) Rohm & Haas Company (*); (*right*) Walter Chandoha (*)
16–17: (*left*) William Bridge, Tom Stack & Associates (*); (*top right*) Warren Garst, Tom Stack & Associates (*), (*bottom right*) Russ Kinne, Photo Researchers (*)
18–19: (*top left*) Warren Garst (*); (*bottom left*) William Vandivert (*), Warren Garst (*); (*top right*) Carleton Ray, Photo Researchers (*), (*center right*) CHILDCRAFT photo by Tor Eigeland, (*bottom right*) Warren Garst (*)
20–21: (*top left*) Walter Rohdich, APF (*), (*center left*) Anthony Mercieca, NAS, (*), Glen Sherwood (*), (*bottom left*) Nelson Medina, Burton McNeely Photography (*); (*top right*) Lars Christiansen, APF (*), (*bottom right*) Dan Gibson, Miller Services (*)
22–23: (*top left*) R. F. Head, NAS (*), (*bottom left*) Robert Hermes, APF (*), (*top right*) Stephen Collins, Photo Researchers (*), (*bottom right*) Warren Garst (*), Jane Burton, Photo Researchers (*)
24–25: (*top left*) Warren Garst (*), (*bottom left*) Tom Mc-Hugh, Photo Researchers (*); (*top right*) Russ Kinne, Photo Researchers (*), (*center right*) Noble Proctor, Photo Researchers (*), (*bottom right*) C. E. Mohr, NAS (*)
26–27: George Lopac
28–29: Norman Weaver
30–31: G. J. Chafaris (*)
32–33: (*left*) J. M. Conrader (*); (*right*) George P. Miller, Black Star (*)
34–35: (*left*) W. Brindle, Australian News and Information Bureau (*); (*right*) Grant Thomson, APF (*), Jack Dermid (*)
36–37: (*left*) Don Moss; (*right*) Wallace Kirkland (*)
38–39: (*left*) Norman Weaver; (*right*) Edward Slater (*), Helen Cruickshank, NAS (*)
40–41: (*left*) Bernhard Grzimek, Okapia (*); (*right*) Norman Weaver
42–43: (*left*) Norman Weaver; (*top right*) James Loy, Van Cleve Photography (*), Eric Hosking (*), (*bottom right*) S. C. Bisserot, Bruce Coleman Ltd. (*), Tom McHugh, Photo Researchers (*)
44–45: Betty Fraser
46–47: (*top left*) Stephen Herrero (*), (*bottom left*) Tom Mc-Hugh, Photo Researchers (*); (*top and bottom right*) Tom McHugh, Photo Researchers (*), (*center right*) Stephen Herrero (*)

48–49: (*top and center*) Les Blacklock (*), (*bottom*) Warren Garst (*)
50–51: Guy Tudor
52–53: Russ Kinne, Photo Researchers (*)
54–55: Arthur Twomey, Photo Researchers (*)
56–57: (*left*) G. Ronald Austing (*); (*right*) Guy Tudor
58–59: (*top*) G. Ronald Austing, NAS (*), (*bottom*) Pictorial Parade (*)
60–61: (*left*) Betty Fraser; (*top right*) Bradley Smith, Photo Researchers (*), G. Ronald Austing (*), (*center right*) John C. Schmid, Photo Researchers (*), Sandy Sprunt, NAS (*), (*bottom right*) R. F. Head, NAS (*), Perry Covington, Tom Stack & Associates (*)
62–63: (*top left*) Roy Pinney, Photo-Library (*), (*center left*) Grant Heilman (*), Ann Brewster; (*top right*) Wallace Kirkland, *Life* © Time Inc. (*), (*center right*) Ann Brewster, (*bottom right*) American Museum of Natural History (*)
64–65: Glen Sherwood (*)
66–67: Glen Sherwood (*)
68–69: Norman Weaver
70–71: Russ Kinne, Photo Researchers (*)
72–73: Jane Burton, Bruce Coleman Ltd. (*)
74–75: (*left*) Marineland of Florida (*); (*right*) Laurence Perkins (*)
76–77: (*top*) Peter R. Gimbel (*), (*bottom*) Norman Weaver
78–79: Norman Weaver
80–81: (*top*) Wometco Miami Seaquarium (*), (*bottom*) Ron Church (*)
82–83: Harry McNaught
84–85: G. Ronald Austing (*)
86–87: (*top left*) American Museum of Natural History (*), (*bottom left*) Lewis Walker, Photo Researchers (*); (*top right*) Hal H. Harrison, NAS (*), Lynn Pelham, Rapho Guillumette (*)
88–89: Harry McNaught
90–91: (*top*) Leonard Lee Rue, APF (*), (*bottom*) Don Carr, Tom Stack & Associates (*)
92–93: (*top*) Wide World (*), (*center and bottom*) San Diego Zoo photo by Ron Garrison (*)
94–95: Robert E. Lunt, APF (*)
96–97: Harry McNaught
98–99: Harry McNaught
100–101: Walter Rohdich, APF (*)
102–103: (*top left*) G. Ronald Austing (*), (*bottom left*) W. Mahoney, Shostal Associates (*); (*top right*) E. R. Degginger (*), (*center right*) Leonard Lee Rue, APF (*), (*bottom right*) G. Ronald Austing (*)
104–105: (*top*) Jane Burton, Bruce Coleman Ltd. (*), (*bottom*) George Porter, NAS (*)
106–107: Harry McNaught
108–109: (*top left*) S. C. Bisserot, Photo Researchers (*), (*center and bottom left*) Jane Burton, Photo Researchers (*); (*top right*) Jane Burton, Photo Researchers (*), (*bottom right*) James H. Keller (*)
110–111: Walter Linsenmaier
112–113: (*top left*) Lia Munson (*), (*bottom left*) Betty Fraser; (*top right*) A. W. Cooper, Photo Researchers (*), (*bottom right*) Hermann Eisenbeiss, Photo Researchers (*)
114–115: (*top left*) Otto W. Wehrle, Photo Researchers (*), (*bottom left*) John H. Gerard, NAS (*); (*top right*) Richard Parker, DPI (*), (*bottom right*) Betty Fraser
116–117: (*left*) Walter Linsenmaier; (*top right*) Walter Dawn (*), (*bottom right*) Betty Fraser
118–119: (*top*) Treat Davidson, Photo Researchers (*), (*center*) Annan Photo (*), (*bottom*) Syd Greenberg, Photo Researchers (*)
120–121: (*left*) Alexander B. Klots (*), S. C. Bisserot, Bruce Coleman Ltd. (*); (*right*) Alexander B. Klots (*), S. C. Bisserot, Bruce Coleman Ltd. (*)
122–123: Edward S. Ross
124–125: (*top*) Jack Dermid, NAS (*), (*center and bottom*) Ross E. Hutchins (*)
126–127: (*top left*) Treat Davidson, NAS (*), (*center left*) Jerome Wexler, Photo Researchers (*), (*bottom left*) Phillippe Scott, Photo Researchers (*); (*top right*) Arthur W. Ambler, NAS (*), (*bottom right*) Larry West, NAS (*)
128–129: (*left*) Walter Linsenmaier; (*top right*) Walter Linsenmaier, (*bottom right*) Walter Dawn (*)
130–131: Walter Linsenmaier
132–133: Walter Linsenmaier
134–135: G. Ronald Austing (*)

136–137: *(left and right)* Douglas Faulkner (*)
138–139: *(top left)* George Lower (*), *(bottom left)* Terry Shaw, APF (*); *(right)* Darrell Ward, Tom Stack & Associates (*)
140–141: D. P. Wilson, F.R.P.S., Marine Biological Laboratory, Plymouth, England (*)
142–143: Walter Linsenmaier
144–145: *(top left)* Betty Fraser, *(bottom)* Walter Linsenmaier
146–147: *(top left)* N. J. Berrill (*), *(bottom left)* Russ Kinne, Photo Researchers (*); *(top right)* Allan Power, Bruce Coleman Ltd. (*), *(bottom right)* B. Bartram Cadbury, NAS (*)
148–149: Lou Bory Associates
150–151: *(top and center)* Runk/Schoenberger, Grant Heilman Photography (*), *(bottom)* Walter Dawn (*)
152–153: *(left)* Runk/Schoenberger, Grant Heilman Photography (*); *(right)* Eric V. Grave' (*)
154–155: Eric V. Grave' (*)
156–157: Betty Fraser
158–159: Norman Weaver
160–161: *(top)* Jane P. Downton, Tom Stack & Associates (*), *(bottom)* Lia Munson (*), Eric Hosking (*)
162–163: Lilo Hess, Three Lions (*)
164–165: *(top)* H. Root, Okapia (*), *(bottom)* Karl H. Maslowski (*)
166–167: *(left)* American Museum of Natural History (*); *(right)* Karl H. Maslowski (*), James Simon, Photo Researchers (*)
168–169: Mark Boulton, NAS (*)
170–171: James Simon, Photo Researchers (*)
172–173: Norman Weaver
174–175: Animals, Animals (*)
176–177: *(left)* G. Ronald Austing (*); *(top right)* De Wys, Inc. (*), *(center right)* James Simon, Photo Researchers (*), *(bottom right)* Russ Kinne, Photo Researchers (*)
178–179: *(top right)* Leonard Lee Rue III, Shostal (*), *(bottom right)* Walter Dawn (*)
180–181: Tom Myers (*)
182–183: *(top)* Norman Myers, Photo Researchers (*), *(bottom)* Douglas Faulkner (*)
184–185: *(left)* James Shields, Photo Researchers (*); *(right)* Norman Weaver
186–187: Norman Weaver
188–189: Warren Garst (*)
190–191: Alex Ebel
192–193: *(top left)* C. Robert Lee, Photo Researchers (*), *(bottom left)* Horst Bielfeld, NAS (*); *(top right)* Horst Bielfeld, NAS (*), *(center and bottom right)* M. W. F. Tweedie, NAS (*)
194–195: *(left)* Alex Ebel; *(right)* Russ Kinne, Photo Researchers (*)
196–197: *(top left)* Karl Maslowski (*), *(bottom left)* Raymond A. Mendez, Photo Trends (*); *(right)* Louis Quitt, Photo Researchers (*)
198–199: *(left)* Alex Ebel; *(right)* National Communicable Disease Center (*)
200–201: Willis Peterson (*)
202–203: *(left)* Willis Peterson (*); *(right)* Carleton Ray, Photo Researchers (*)
204–205: *(right)* Norman Myers, Photo Researchers (*), E. R. Degginer (*)
206–207: *(left)* Douglas Baglin Photography, Pty., Ltd., NAS (*); *(right)* Russ Kinne, Photo Researchers (*)
208–209: *(left)* Van Nostrand Photo, NAS (*); *(right)* Leonard Lee Rue, III, NAS (*)
210–211: *(left)* John Moyer, NAS (*); *(right)* Russ Kinne, Photo Researchers (*)
212–213: Betty Fraser
214–215: Harry McNaught
216–217: H. Doering, APF (*)
218–219: Norman Myers, Photo Researchers (*)
220–221: Harry McNaught
222–223: *(top)* Tom W. Hall (*), *(bottom)* Russ Kinne, Photo Researchers (*)
224–225: *(right)* G. Ronald Austing, NAS (*)
226–227: Harry McNaught
228–229: Syd Greenberg, Photo Researchers (*)
230–231: *(top)* Maurice Wilson, *(bottom)* U.S. Army (*)
232–233: Alex Ebel
234–235: *(left)* Mas Nakagawa; *(right)* Alex Ebel
236–237: *(left)* Alex Ebel; *(right)* Mas Nakagawa
238–239: *(left)* Mas Nakagawa; *(right)* Alex Ebel

240–241: Alex Ebel
242–243: Alex Ebel
244–245: Alex Ebel
246–247: Alex Ebel
248–249: Alex Ebel
250–251: *(top)* Russ Kinne, Photo Researchers (*), *(bottom)* Laurence Pringle, NAS (*)
252–253: Alex Ebel
254–255: Alex Ebel
256–257: Peter Barrett
258–259: *(top left)* Alan Band Associates (*), *(bottom left)* CHILDCRAFT photo by Flip Schulke, Black Star; *(right)* CHILDCRAFT photos by Flip Schulke, Black Star
260–261: CHILDCRAFT photos by Flip Schulke, Black Star
262–263: CHILDCRAFT photos by Flip Schulke, Black Star
264–265: CHILDCRAFT photos by Flip Schulke, Black Star
266–267: *(top left)* Donald S. Sade, Van Cleve Photography (*), *(center left)* Glen Sherwood (*), *(bottom left)* George Holton, Photo Researchers (*); *(top and bottom right)* Flip Schulke, Black Star (*)
268–269: *(left)* Wisconsin Regional Primate Research Center (*); *(top right)* Russ Kinne, Photo Researchers (*), *(bottom right)* Harry Redl, Black Star (*)
270–271: *(top left)* Photoreporters, Inc., (*), *(center left)* Marc & Evelyne Bernheim, Rapho Guillumette (*), *(bottom left)* Terence Spencer, Black Star (*); *(right)* Patricia Caulfield, Rapho Guillumette (*)
272–273: *(left)* Hazelton Laboratories, Inc. (*); *(top right)* Dan Bernstein, Photo Researchers (*), *(bottom right)* Gerge Whiteley, Photo Researchers (*)
274–275: *(top left)* CHILDCRAFT photo by Virginia Eckelberry, *(bottom left)* CHILDCRAFT photo by Bernard Photographers; *(right)* reproduction of painting "Bobwhite" by Don Richard Eckelberry © Frame House Gallery, Louisville, Ky.
276–277: Robert J. Lee
278–279: *(left)* H. Armstrong Roberts (*); *(right)* Jerry Frank, DPI (*)
280–281: *(top)* Grant Heilman (*), *(center)* Marty Reker, Photo Researchers (*); *(bottom)* Grant Heilman (*), Walter Chandoha (*)
282–283: *(top left)* Herb and Dorothy McLaughlin (*), *(bottom left)* Miller Services (*); *(right)* Joe Monroe, Photo Researchers (*)
284–285: *(left)* A. M. Wettach (*); *(top right)* Grant Heilman (*), *(bottom right)* Bart Jarner
286–287: *(top left)* CHILDCRAFT photo, *(bottom left)* Roland and Sabrina Michaud, Rapho Guillumette (*); *(right)* George Lopac
288–289: *(top left)* Pilot Guide Dog Foundation (*), *(bottom left)* Bart Jarner; *(top right)* Bart Jarner, *(bottom right)* Franklin Photo (*)
290–291: *(left)* Walter Chandoha (*); *(top right)* Stephen Collins NAS (*), Treat Davidson, NAS (*), *(bottom right)* Joe Munroe, Photo Researchers (*), Sybil Shackman, Monkmeyer (*)
292–293: *(left)* Miller Services (*); *(top right)* T. S. Nagarajan, Miller Services (*), *(center right)* Miller Services (*), *(bottom right)* Paolo Koch, Photo Researchers (*)
294–295: Peter Barrett
296–297: *(top left)* Graham Young, Photo Trends (*), *(bottom left)* Mark N. Boulton, NAS (*); *(top right)* Dr. Georg Gerster, Rapho Guillumette (*), *(bottom right)* CHILDCRAFT photo by Ray Halin
298–299: *(left)* CHILDCRAFT photo by Weston Kemp; *(right)* John Neel, Tom Stack & Associates (*)
300–301: *(top left)* Publix Pictorial (*), *(bottom left)* Al Satterwhite, Camera 5 (*) Cyril Maitland, Camera 5 (*); *(top right and bottom)* Lynn Pelham, Rapho Guillumette (*)
302–303: *(top left)* von Meiss-Teuffen, Photo Researchers (*), *(bottom left)* Bradley Smith, Photo Researchers (*); *(right)* Norman Myers, Photo Researchers (*)
304–305: Betty Fraser
306–307: Betty Fraser
308–309: Betty Fraser
310–311: Betty Fraser
312–313: Betty Fraser
314–315: Betty Fraser
316–317: Betty Fraser
318–319: Betty Fraser
320–321: Betty Fraser

Index

This index can help you find the pages that tell about each animal. For example, if you want to find the pages that tell about elephants, look under Elephant. This listing includes the pages that tell about African elephants, baby elephants, extinct elephants, Indian elephants, and elephants' tails and trunks.

Maybe you want to find a certain animal but you can't remember its exact name. If you know to which class it belongs—amphibian, arthropod, bird, fish, mammal, or reptile—you can look under that class. For example, you'll find Canada goose listed under Bird.